Table of Contents

Barracking from the Sidelines 2014

(My personal political commentary on politicians and political events in 2014)

By Greg Tuck

Preface

Australian Politics

Dominated by a federal government, in a three-tier system of government, Australian politics is based on a constitution written in the 1890's that is extremely difficult to change via referendums. It is a Westminster system of government that has two separate chambers that are dominated by two major parties whose ideologies differ and both the sides are very combative to the extent that agreement on issues except politician wage increase, are hard won battles. If one side thinks of an idea, the other side shoots it down in flames, whether the idea is good or not. The public have become disillusioned and feel impotent to change things and see most politicians as merely sucking on the public teat and lining their own pockets. A good few of the political rank's behaviour does nothing to dispel that idea.

Politics changed a lot in Australia from late 2013 onwards, although many will attest to the fact that it hasn't changed at all. There are still lies, deception, obfuscation and manipulation and these have had to become more sophisticated as social media has come to the fore. I have been adding my own comments to mainstream media and my own political blog in those years and on reflection I am amazed at the types of characters that are regularly unearthed and come to the forefront in our political climate.

Some characters have developed over that time. Some were just fleeting shadows on the political spectrum. Others rose from obscurity and some may have also have faded back into it. Characters and events overlap. Views change and political manoeuvres take place. Ideology dictates much of what goes on. Hopefully my blog entries and reflections will help paint a picture of these characters and events that dominated the political scene in this period. This is not a chronological history of the time, merely one person's thoughts that he wanted to scream at the major players in Australian politics at the time.

However, the disappointing thing about all these comments and research is what I still really don't understand is, how does the Canberra bubble still remain intact with so many pricks in it? Are there special properties of moral vacuums?

January

- Major bushfires in Victoria, WA and Queensland
- Fruit packaging company not given assistance funding by Federal Government

I am hoping that Abbott won't implode because the people of Australia deserve a government that is all about making the right decisions on behalf of them and not on their own self-interest. That's what happened when Kevin started losing the plot and had to be replaced. he was elected not as a king but as a leader of a team. He had a great team. I don't agree with a lot of Abbott's policies especially on asylum seekers, the environment, education etc. But I don't agree with the country being run by people who can't work together and won't stand by their principles.

We have seen the petulant Tony dragging around his lip on the floor of Parliament after he lost the last election. Can we now see the magnanimous Tony after this victory? Australians have high hopes that Tony can "Stop the Gloats!"

Our fire service and SES only get some recognition when there is a catastrophic event. The most lucrative financial rewards are given to our entertainers and sportsmen. Little value is placed on service workers such as nurses, police and teachers who, given their pay, can't be in it for the money. Yet they are often the brunt of criticism when a government wants to lay blame when things go wrong. The media investigate mistakes, highlight them, twist them, spin them and when wrong print a retraction buried amongst a range of less newsworthy items. We champion the freedom of the press but the media and its commercial culture tell us what to buy, who to vote for, who is "good" and who is "evil", what's important and what to think. We say we are in an information overload but that information is being carefully screened to present a viewpoint.

Is the media a servant or a master? Who is in control of what we see hear and think? A soldier has been killed in Afghanistan and his death will make headlines for a day or so. Two celebrities have a little little dalliance and it becomes front page news for a week. Which is more newsworthy? Which affects us more? Somewhere; someone has made that decision on our behalf.

We owe a lot to the people who came before us for making this country what it is today. Sadly, the choice of the 26th of January reminds us of things like racism, terra nullius, invasion, racism and colonialism still symbolised by the Union Jack in the corner of our own flag. Perhaps that is a good thing, so that we can learn from the past. If the indigenous people of Australia in 1788 had the same asylum seeker policy we have today, then what we have now would be vastly different. Immigrants such as Tony Abbott might then know what it feels like to risk everything to seek a better, safer and more prosperous life, only to be turned back, sent overseas or incarcerated like too many of today's would-be Australians.

People are finally talking about global warming and climate change. Australia is a place of "droughts and flooding rains" yet we continue to farm the land as if it wasn't. We till the soil until the nutrients are depleted and topsoil is cast to the wind. We irrigate until the land is turned into salt plains. We fertilise until we kill off the reefs and damage the ecosystems there as chemicals leach into the oceans. We certainly aren't the "clever country" are we?

Farmers complain about the lack of rain and banks swoop in as mortgages can't be paid. How have we addressed the issue? Possibly by burying our heads in the sand that threatens to envelop the continent in years to come. If crops fail year after year, are we growing the wrong crops? If cattle and sheep are over-grazing land, are they the most suitable livestock to use given our climate? Have we looked at what countries with similar conditions are growing or raising successfully? When we have to buy our way into markets and farmers in the long term at best only break even, does anyone stop to think that something is wrong? Perhaps we should grow enough wheat, beef and lamb for domestic consumption and search for different export markets for other products.

Forget the Awesome Foursome and Steve Redgrave, the greatest most erudite rower ever is to be found in Robert Bolt's "A Man for All Seasons". His comment about being paid the same whether he rows upstream or downstream puts him a clear canvas ahead of the rest. When we dictate a person's pay based on incorrect, ill-informed and ill-conceived data we fall into the trap of being a data driven workforce. In teaching you can work smart and work your backside off with little progress in a school where the odds are heavily stacked against kids making "substantial" gains in learning outcomes. There are predominantly more ethnicity problems, behaviour management concerns, transient enrolments, health issues, low socio-economic related inhibitors etc. that you have to row against. Yet the notion of performance-based pay for teachers would reward those who are in schools downstream. The children in those schools are already advantaged and if performance-based pay comes in as state and federal coalition parties want, the best rowers will opt to row downstream. There is a clear relationship between rowing and performance pay for teachers. You will achieve more as a team all pulling in unison in the one direction, but it is much harder and more of a challenge to row upstream. But politicians, coaching from the sidelines, see only the flat surface where all things appear equal but ignore the tidal movements, the undercurrents and eddies and the snags. Perhaps they should talk to the rowing crews who are battling these and going upstream.

With welfare and taxation arguments are raised and data is carefully selected, there does seem to be an imbalance doesn't there. But how would the bottom four fifths survive without support? When the vast majority of people are not contributing to the effective tax pool they are probably not earning enough. Wages are suppressed so they can't contribute more. This leaves the top fifth to make more profit and then complain about the amount of money they have to contribute to the taxation pool. Capitalism will always breed the haves and have nots. It's inbuilt in the structural mechanism. Taxation is a lever that is used to control the disparity. Otherwise workers would just down tools and the whole system would fall over. Historical evidence confirms this. So perhaps the top fifth should just live with it and realise they can't have their cake and eat it too. At least they have cake............ a la Marie Antoinette. It all comes down to opportunities. Taxation helps to equalise some of the opportunities through health education etc. Without that the top fifth would not have workers to help their businesses remaining in profit.

"The real long-term winner will be Bill Shorten. To get the top job in Labour, he had to see Gillard go, even though she had done a fantastic job managing a hung parliament. Combet, his main long-term rival, disappear off the scene. Penny Wong, the shining light for Labour stay in the Senate and then Rudd to fall flat on his face in an election. Shorten can wear the NDIS as a badge of honour quite justifiably. He will also take credit for negotiating deals on Gillard's education reforms because that dud Peter Garrett couldn't strike deals. Yes, Shorten is the real long term winner just as Turnbull is the long-term loser for the Coalition. If Labour had won, the roles would be reversed between the two."

"When you see the news out of Canberra each day there is another stunning revelation. Today's, that Tony Abbott wants to be notified before any Ministers speak in public, sounds like damage control to me.

The damage so far:

* Julie Bishop (The only female found worthy to be in cabinet) offending Indonesia by telling them what Australia will do inside Indonesia's sovereign borders, and as possible chairperson of UN

Security Council pre-empting what the response to the Syrian situation should be.

* Christopher Pyne looking at caps on Uni positions when he said he wouldn't just prior to the election

* Scott Morrison saying that "operational matters" will reduce the dissemination about information about asylum seeker boats

* Joe Hockey admitting that the government will need to spend to assist fiscal growth and contradicting Andrew Robb's views

* Malcolm Turnbull sacking and then stacking the NBN board

* Bronwyn Bishop, neutral Speaker elect for house of Reps, expressing very one-sided view on what could and shouldn't be said in parliament. i.e. that Tony's put downs were fair and Gillard's responses were not.

* Peter Dutton commenting on the Essendon drugs saga

* Greg Hunt's comments about the Climate Commission and that it shouldn't have been publicly funded in the first place

* Barnaby Joyce for just opening his mouth

* Deciding to have a Sports Minister but no Science Minister

Will Tony be the calming influence that gets all these egos to go in the one direction or will he have to resort to bullying tactics to quell the infighting?

Whichever way, it will be an interesting but bumpy ride."

In 2010 Victorians elected a Liberal Government to be led by Ted Baillieu. They were elected on a platform of major infrastructure promises including train lines to Doncaster, Rowville, Melbourne Airport and Avalon airport. All were seen as priorities not only by Victorian and the Liberal Government, but also Infrastructure Australia. A coup occurred and Dennis Napthine replaced Ted Baillieu and suddenly Victorians were facing a different transport proposal that they hadn't voted for. Contracts will be signed before the next election and Victorians will be saddled with massive major road (not rail) "improvements".

Because of confidentiality Victorians will not see the business case, the major benefits outlined in that case and the evidence that supports those benefits. The deceit that is being practised on the Victorian electors shows how little the current government values promises and exemplifies their "born to rule" mentality. If they had more dignity than gall, they would take their plans to the next election and get a mandate. They won't and it will be too late by then. State Liberals cling to power with the aid of a now independent member who is facing criminal charges. It is time that Victorians re-examined the political promises outlined in the 2010 election. It is time to say "No" to policies that weren't outlined in that election platform. It is time that governments were held to account. It is time that all political parties stopped treating their electorates with disdain. The people of Victoria did not give a carte blanche and blank cheque at the last election. Governments need to honour their major promises or at the very least explain why those promises couldn't be met. They need to take those changes back to the public via an election and seek a mandate. The State Liberal Government has broken its contract with Victoria. What a shame this "board of directors" can't be charged with fraud.

The French Revolution is a perfect example of the throwing out of an oppressive regime. It was an economic awakening by the French that the divide between rich and poor had become too vast. Not even the soothing of religion could pacify the poor. Over time religious orders have become the tool of the wealthy by keeping people in place and giving them hope of a better "after-life" as this one is so sh!t. Marx was right when he (and I paraphrase this) said "Religion is the opiate of the masses" In other words it is used to dull aspirations, hide the truth and raise the profile of the religious order and the wealthy. Because the two groups, the rich and the religious leaders have worked hand in glove throughout history from prehistoric times, they have amassed power and influence. The only threats they have are education and science.

Science will disprove a lot of the religious teachings that have made the population docile, and education will allow the masses to have a far clearer view of the world. Issues have arisen when the religious and economic world have clashed as instead of working together, they have fought each other to establish superiority. The Reformation was a great example. The division of the church in Henry VIII's time. The demise of the Shah of Iran. The rise of Mao in China. The end of the monarchy in Russia.

It is the power that comes from economic control supported by the religious orders that cause the major conflicts in the world, not just religion alone. How many revolutions have occurred where there is a good balance between the rich and the poor? How many extremist elements get to create havoc when a country has that balance right? By getting rid of Saddam, all the west did was create a power vacuum and some religious zealots have taken control. It was predictable. For a supposedly educated lot the leaders of the coalition of the willing were as thick as two planks. Instead of bombing the hell out of a country spend the money on creating wealth within the masses. This is the safest and most effective way to do it. By raising the standard of living in a country then that prosperity will bring security, and security will allow for education and science to flourish, and that in turn will prevent religious and political extremists from taking a grip. But the western world won't do that. They must protect their own interests first including oil security and maintaining their arms manufacturing. The latter means that there must be conflict somewhere or else that industry goes under. We didn't intervene and Rwanda and Eritrea where even greater internal conflict and genocide occurred because there was no money in it. Why is Mugabe still in power..........? Zimbabwe is poor and if a country is poor and likely to remain so then there are no arms sales.

The job of a leader whether a political or religious leader (or both) is to convince and promise the plebs that they can have everything. It is when the plebs realise that what they say is a complete crock then major conflicts begin. That is why education can be seen as dangerous. (Just a thought.... maybe that is why Manus Island and Nauru are in the cone of silence.) That is why religious and wealthy people do not want it for the masses. It is a threat to their power base. When the west invaded Iraq and toppled Saddam they offered a western style democracy to a group of people who had no experience of it and who found that there were no real benefits as their lives were suddenly harsher. Of course, they turned to leaders who promised more. If the western nations had offered democracy and economic stability the situation would have been much better.

Cuba was no accident. Castro offered hope when there was none. Mao offered hope, Lenin offered hope, Hitler offered hope.

And what does Tony offer? ... Hype!

People blame religion for all the world's ills but it is a worship of money and power that is the main cause. Those with wealth want to keep it. Those without, want to have it. When there is such a divide between rich and poor, then there is potential for conflict. Powerful leaders through time have kept their populations ignorant by keeping them uneducated. They have kept them in line by sedating them with religion. Extremism whether aligned to a religion or not festers in such an environment. It offers hope where there is none. Instead of invading and imposing a western democracy, think of the benefits of spending some of the massive amount of money being spent currently on armaments, being targeted on raising the standard of living and education in poorer countries. If only. But then the munitions industry would go broke and where would we be?

February

- **More bushfires in Victoria**
- **Ebola virus epidemic in West Africa begins, infecting at least 28,616 people and killing at least 11,310 people, the most severe both in terms of numbers of infections and casualties.**
- **Belgium becomes the first country in the world to legalise euthanasia for terminally ill patients of any age.**
- **The Verkhovna Rada (Ukrainian parliament) votes to remove President Viktor Yanukovych from office, replacing him with Oleksandr Turchynov, after days of civil unrest leaving around 100 people dead in Kiev**

It is believed that, having a Westminster system of government, with its governing body and opposition, serious debate will take place and policies and their accompanying legislation will be rigorously scrutinized, so what is finally enacted will be as good as it possibly can be. However, in a party-political system such as we have, many politicians would be better off leaving their egos at the door along with their outside affiliations and schoolyard mentality, and bring inside the halls of government their ideals, their aspirations for the country and the representative viewpoint of their electorate. Some justify what they do and say under what is called parliamentary privilege, but many often seem not to respect the privilege that they have been given to be in parliament in the first place.

Man has not come all that far since, as a wild animal, he hunted in packs with club and spear. Wars over the years have been won or lost on that same premise. The game has been fostered over the years in acceptance of schoolyard bullying, racism, xenophobia etc. and is almost enshrined in the leadership we see in parliament. There is no new paradigm. To have that, there needs a huge shift in the culture of the parliament itself and that takes time and a will. We have seen in the past weeks how two schoolyard gangs work. The Liberal gang had to depose Malcolm the Likeable as he was not making inroads against the Milky Bar Kid. In his stead they put forward Tony the Taunter who sensed a weakness and went for the jugular. The Milky Bar Kid lacked assurance and faltered. The Labour gang then had the choice of giving ground or putting up someone else to take on Tony the Taunter, and the rest is history.

Just as the last major change in the global climate killed off the dinosaurs, the internet will kill off the media dinosaurs such as newspapers and so-called current affair television. Journalists such as Andrew Bolt proselytising about his opinion about global warming will suffer a similar fate. With his head buried in the sand, who will hear him?

I am a bit concerned that we think we live in a democracy. We can't freely choose who to vote for. Because of the party system, candidates for areas are preselected and often parachuted in. Money flows freely in to the larger parties so an independent has to compete with outside interests backing a party candidate. We think we can vote for a prime minister but the party with the majority forms a government and elects the prime minister. So, in effect voters choose the least worst person to represent them and out of all of those elected half of them choose the least worst as prime minister, who then makes sure that those who donated heavily to his/her party get something in return.

Inclination - uphill or downhill? We say it is an uphill battle to achieve anything so why is the saying it is all downhill from here as we sink into the mire.

Reality - well it just sucks according to the politicians but they know nothing of reality. Canberra is an alternate universe. Though we may declare they are "out of this world", that is merely an aspiration rather than a compliment.

It still comes down to the way the government has always been run. It is a Westminster system of basically two parties who white ant each other to get to the top. Some individuals white ant their own party. Australians really have only two choices at the ballot box and choose the lesser of two evils. The power of the vote is in the preselection and that is done by a few. So, we get whatever a faction or alignment decide is the candidate. That's why really good people don't go into government. If you were running a business would you want so many black hat thinkers around you as there are in Parliament. Your business would be dysfunctional........... like our government. Your business would be insolvent......... like our government. Your business would cease to exist.......... unlike our government who slash services or raise taxes to hide their ineptitude. For God's sake they treat the whole thing as a game!!!!

What is wealth? What should it be defined as? Wealth has always been associated with money. Real wealth is more to do with power and influence and this occurs at many levels many of which are not financially rewarding. A great idea put forward by someone on the factory floor that gets enacted and boosts a company's profits by 5% may be given a bonus, but each one up the food chain will also get a bonus for passing on the idea. The difference being that a 2% bonus on the factory floor is far less than the CEO who also gets a 2% bonus. The shareholders may get an extra 3% but they have achieved that based on the thoughts and ideas of a person who may be slung $10 extra a week. These anomalies exist and a good CEO would backtrack to where the actual idea came from and give credit where it is due.

Governments should do the same. They have this pool of money garnished from all and sundry and yet they spend it on things people don't need, people don't want and all because they can. They redistribute the wealth of the citizens based on postcodes within electorates. We are a common-wealth yet certain electorates are

uncommonly wealthy. Should those who contribute more receive more, be forced to pay more or pay equal or less than others. A flat tax such as the GST hits everyone the same. The only difference is that the less affluent you are, the less you have left over to spend on necessities.

If you accept that nurses, social workers etc. contribute a whole lot of wealth to the society but they don't raise money, make profits or have difficulty trying to demonstrate their economic benefit; does this mean what they do is less valued? It is as far as wages are concerned. Someone who gambles other people's money such as stockbrokers, government ministers, bankers etc., should they get paid more or less than a nurse?

It all comes back to what value do you put on a certain person's occupation. In years gone by the night cart person was paid precious little for a dangerous and dirty job that few would do. No-one aspired to be a night cart person. But what if nobody did it? society would have been up the proverbial creek. Night cart people carried a lot on their shoulders, the kind of stuff politicians and barristers speak but they are more valuable to a society.

So perhaps if we re-organised occupations based on the actual contribution to society and paid them accordingly, then it may be the top current 5th who may be needing welfare.

The Greens may not have lost their focus but have lost their capacity to intellectually convey their message. Bob Brown had the personality and capability to articulate the major thrust of the Greens. Without him there, there is a loss of credence and his replacement has fallen into the trap of becoming as politically supple as the Libs and Labour so the party doesn't have that forward-thinking anti-establishment image it once had. That is why strength and vigour isn't there in terms of public perception and that is what counts.... public perception reflected in the ballot box.

March

- Royal Commission into Trade Union Governance and Corruption begins
- Prime Minister Tony Abbott reintroduces the titles of knights and dames into the Order of Australia honours list.
- Malaysia Airlines Flight 370, a Boeing 777 airliner en route to Beijing from Kuala Lumpur, disappears over the Gulf of Thailand with 239 people on board.
- Russia formally annexes Crimea.
- Russia is suspended from the G8
- The UN International Court of Justice rules that Japan's Antarctic whaling program is not scientific but commercial and forbids grants of further permits

After the great speech by Rachel Griffiths on Q & A last night about the standards of behaviour we should expect in question time and in parliament in general, she must be feeling it fell on deaf ears.

When you ask parents what they want for their child at school, the vast majority have high in their priorities, happiness and friendship. Yes, they want them to read, write, spell, do maths, be computer literate and at the end of their schooling be educated enough to get a job, preferably in a career of their choice. It is a shame that education has become mired in the assessment of the three r's. For students that stifles happiness, learning growth and often pits one child against another. Children work cooperatively on joint projects with others and learn to value each other's strengths and limitations. When it comes to assessment however, that goes out the window.

Russell Broadbent are you aware of the lies, deceit, secrecy and abuse of power that are occurring on your watch as a representative of

McMillan? People should be able to seek asylum here and be processed here. It is in the UN Charter to which we have agreed. Either tear up the charter or honour it. Either cross the floor, put up a private members bill or resign. But don't dare to say that we are doing all we can to aid genuine asylum seekers; the so-called "Illegal" who have been incarcerated in overseas concentration camps without trial and having committed no crime.

The US prides itself on democracy and as a leader of the free world but they have an electoral system that is open to flaws and can isolate and marginalize the very best candidates from being president.

Remember the parable of the Good Samaritan who gave help to someone in need despite not knowing them? In less than a month we celebrate the birth of Christ who related that parable Anyone so desperate to go on an unseaworthy boat to Australia, risking everything seems to be someone in need. Yet according to the high and mighty, the ones who should lead by example, Good Samaritans are just "Humbug".

There is no room at the inn, stable or anywhere in Australia for these people who wish to claim asylum. Instead we turn them away, even though they need our help. Politicians say we do it to stop them drowning in boats and to stop the people smugglers. If we were allowed to be Good Samaritans, we would send a plane and bring them here for free and that too would solve the issues. Instead of showing humanity, we put them through inhumane treatment to protect our wonderful lifestyle and moral certitude.

One wonders if the Virgin Mary, another asylum seeker, had taken a boat to Australia instead of riding a donkey to Bethlehem; would Jesus have been born on the island named after his birthday? Or Nauru? Or Manus Island? Certainly not the Australian mainland; our politicians, smiling with "Humsmugness", would see to that.

Australian society is under a tax from lots of quarters. When you are born there is even a fee charged to be registered for being born. Fees charged for this and that all through your life. You pay taxes on food, entertainment and even earning money. No wonder people try to structure their affairs to pay as little tax as possible or try to claim their reward of a pension for having paid taxes all their lives. After all, they have got nothing back from all their taxes up until then? .... wait a minute. The hospital they were born in, the nurses, the maternal care nurse, kindergarten, schools, roads, footpaths, government, police, defence, disaster relief, emergency services, consular help on overseas trips who paid for that?

I could go on but that may be too taxing for you. If they taxed the air around us, we would feel justified far more about complaining about the quality of the air. Nothing would change except we would blame the government for taking money under false pretences. We live in a society and we do that because a group can achieve more than one individual. As part of that social structure there are expectations of sharing, accepting others, participating and assisting those less fortunate. When we forget that we lose our humanity.

Before you believe the numbers in an opinion poll, it is very important poll that you look at the way the questions were phrased for the poll. Otherwise good pollsters can give you whatever results you'd like by manipulating the questions.

"Nothing in a free society should limit the expression of an opinion. My only criticism is that journalists be they work for Fairfax, Murdoch or anyone else are seen as NEWSpaper reporters but it seems the news items are heavily outweighed by opinion pieces just as the interweb thingy does. Present the facts and let people make up their own mind. Opinion expressed as fact is

deceitful and should be condemned as such. That's my opinion as a matter of fact."

"Do you think that Tony will cut defence spending and merely rely on his Foreign Minister's Death Stare which has now been declared a lethal weapon."

Has anyone noticed that, when using political language, to create the opposite meaning all you have to do is start the word with a capital letter?

Liberal – normally means "open to new ideas" but not so in political speak

Labour – normally means "work" but with a capital letter, now viewed as "doesn't work"

National –normally means "of or for the whole nation" but not with a political capital

Green – normally means "strong and vigorous" – enough said

I tried contacting the opposition by email about this and all I got was the "out of office" reply.

Tony Abbott was apprised of the financial situation through the budget honesty process before the election and yet went ahead with bold promises. Now just six months after the election he claims that there is a substantial deficit and that his promises can't be kept. Either Tony was poorly advised before the election or he is poorly advised now. Couldn't be political though could it? An opposition can promise the world and claim afterwards they didn't know. It seems to me a breach of contract. Can I contact the ACCC or is there someone else I can see to sue the government?

April

- **A loss of 1,375 ballot papers in the 2013 federal election causes a special election to be held for six Senate seats from Western Australia.**
- **US President Barack Obama's new economic sanctions against Russia go into effect**

People agree on a number of things. Climate change is occurring and is not in dispute. The one thing that was in dispute was whether man was the <u>major</u> cause of it. That is irrelevant really because man is the only creature in any position to do something about it. And to spend time arguing about what percentage is attributable to man is wasted time. Time that would be better spent on analysing the best ways that man has at his disposal to mitigate the damage, adapt to the change or possibly stabilise the planet's environment; and then putting in place processes that will ensure a better future than the one that many people predict. The discussion should be on the options that could and should be tried rather on what percentage has been caused by man. Perhaps looking at the fact that climate change is not crap and focusing on what the hell can be done is the next step. I have read Bolt and Monkton and many climate scientists discussion papers and frankly I don't give a damn who caused it. I want to know what mankind can do to cope with it, because I have found out how much a cubit is and if I try to build my ark in my driveway then the neighbours are going to be pretty upset.

If you want someone to see things from your viewpoint then making them feel ignorant, incompetent or ignored isn't the best way to go about it. Whilst you may not wish to stand in another person's shoes for health and tinea reasons, sometimes at least acknowledging rather than dismissing their point of view can help to sway them to your point of view. Finding common points of agreement can lead to a common agreed solution. Sweating over points of disagreement will not. In fact, it will put everyone offside. Our politicians model this latter way so effectively

Science and faith are intertwined because of the inexactitude of both. (may have just made up a new word here). There is nothing wrong with believing in one or the other or a mixture of both as most people do. Believing in nothing is much worse. So get off your high horses or the high pedestals that you have placed yourselves on, recognise the possible validity of each other's points of view, look for points you have in common, agree to disagree if you must, and both seek higher ground (not moral higher ground) because you both acknowledge the world is changing. There is nothing worse than a crusade. Most global conflict has been caused by religious beliefs. Our world is on the brink of a nuclear holocaust because of science. Meanwhile us mere plebs who may want to save rainforests even just for their natural beauty have given up looking for who is at fault........ the people who cut the trees down, the multinationals who are making a fortune, the corrupt politicians who turn a blind eye, the advertising executives who tell us that we need to have new things to keep the economy running or the consumers who blindly accept that the loss of rainforests and global warming is the price paid for a materialistic world.

As for me, I am collecting wood to construct an ark but am unsure of what to protect it from the fire and brimstone that scientific zealots and religious fanatics believe will rain down on us. As I live and breathe, I have just found an early 20th century article on the wonders of asbestos............ gotta get me some of that. Scientists think it is fantastic and even religious leaders are having it put into churches (possibly hedging their own bets).

By the way flat earth society people know there will be no issue with rising sea levels as any excess water will just spill off the edge. I

believe in a round earth just because when I go down to the beach, I notice the tops of women first!

Scientists from all over the world have been trying to create the consummate politician and with clone technology and 3D printing capabilities they are now visiting Australia to fine tune what the politician would be like.

Here are the initial findings.

The politician must have:

* At least two faces

* three deaf ears; one each for criticism, advice and constituents

* another ear to the ground to listen for internal party rumblings

* a blind eye aimed towards anything potentially illegal or incriminating

* an eye out of its socket as the politician must always keep an eye out for an opportunity

* an ego large enough to think everyone beneath him/her is of little consequence

* a nose for trouble but large enough to reach the bottom of the trough

* a good set of teeth for photo opportunities and to lie through

* a vacuous smile

* a jelly like chin so that when asked to take it on the chin, little impression is made

* botoxed forehead so that eyebrows aren't ever raised

* the capacity to fake sincerity

* a mouth that emits words but doesn't say anything

* a large vocabulary that allows variations in three-word slogans

* a thick skin so that any slings and arrows aimed at it don't stick, and nothing can get under it

* a fading memory when it comes to promises and for giving evidence

* a jaundiced view of the world

* a superior sense of him/herself thus avoiding any common sense

* a taste for battle in the cut and thrust of politics

* a strong outward view of the world lest any insight take place

* a good sense of smell to seek out injustice and then profit from it

* shoes that have no base in them as a politician rarely has an inner soul

* Flexible fingers that never get caught in the till but seem to be in every pie.

* An aversion to the truth and answering questions

* Gymnastic skills – e.g able to backflip at a moment's notice

* A wide mouth so that even with one foot in it, non-stop justifying statements can be made

* No self-respect

* A long flexible neck so that the attached head can be buried in the sand

* No taste i.e. inability to taste own verbal diarrhoea and BS that is espoused

* No visible means of support i.e. is spineless, blows in the wind and stands for nothing

* Good bowing and scraping skills to use on political masters, be they in the party or just rich and powerful

* Chameleon qualities – change for any situation and melt into obscurity as the need arises. e.g. when sitting in parliament looks like an empty seat

* Capacity to be voiceless when raising issues of importance to own constituents

* A "party" animal demeanour

As you can see the list is quite complex and nowhere near complete. Certain Australian politicians seem to have nearly all of these qualities but none are the perfect politician. Scientists are wondering whether it would be easier to simply clone the indifferent, long suffering, apathetic

Australian population who keep electing these sort of people and then using cloned Australians to populate the world.

It seems Victoria is open for business but in a fire-sale and no-rules apply way. Matthew Guy has rezoned and sold off land to aid the building and construction companies. Terry Mulder has revamped the Melbourne metro project so that infrastructure can service new high-rise developments to the detriment of existing suburbs. He has also put in the East-West link contracts to assist the trucking industry. Now Dennis Napthine has caved in on building reforms thus allowing bad builders to continue to trade. Is there anything that this government won't do to assist business and commercial development? One would have thought that the government's role was to plan and oversee and regulate growth in the best interests of the whole community and not just the business community. Maybe the next election slogan for the government will be "Trust Dennis Napthine? - Shaw can't!"

Well Tony Abbott has solved the issue of us dying from climate change causes. He has committed a paltry amount to fighting the ebola virus and billions making us a target for extremists. If we don't die from extremism, then ebola will get us before the sea levels can rise.

Ted promised that if he was elected Premier of Victoria in 2010, he would not spend millions on political advertising, he would invest in public transport including the metro tunnel, the Doncaster and Airport train lines and... and......... the problem is not that we believed Ted and he was elected. The problem is that we didn't elect Denis as Premier and he doesn't have to honour Ted's promises.

I am happy to admit my ignorance regarding the Islamification of western Judaeo-Christian society and the conflict and misapprehension that is occurring. I don't think that the continual us vs them response by both "sides" is the answer. The power of imams over their congregation is immense and what I find disconcerting is that the

95% of forward-thinking moderate Muslims don't publicly rail against the extremists who hold sway and saturate the news. We all fear what we don't know or understand and as much as my knowledge of Islam is theoretical and my belief that people should be assessed as individuals, I am happy to listen to arguments from people who have been there. As an individual I have never been or felt threatened by a Muslim so I don't know. As a teacher I have taught Muslims and met with their parents but that is an artificial situation. I found them respectful and appreciative of what was being done for them. So you see my experience apart from reading is limited. I have friends who have also taught and lived in Islamic countries who also have had good experiences so maybe I am naïve. What I don't think will work is giving extremists on all sides the power and media focus they desire. Bombing the crap out of a nation is not a solution. It entrenches those extremists in power. Looting a country economically doesn't help either. I don't profess to have a solution. I know that mankind fears what it doesn't know or understand and that extremist elements in any group, race or religion are happy to exploit that. Keeping people poor and uneducated also are means of setting up a cultural divide. A religion that says that another religion must convert to the "one true religion" (and Islam and Christianity both do that) preys upon the intimidated and uneducated. If we were to nuke all the extremists into oblivion, there would be explosions all over the planet, not just in mosques and the Middle East.

May

- **Horror federal budget announced with major changes to welfare. Treasurer Hockey speaks of 'lifters not leaners' and then is caught smoking cigars with finance minister Mathias Cormann afterwards.**

Is question time worth it? Dorothy Dix gets to ask and have answered in full her questions and any from the cross benches or the Opposition get no proper answers or derided by the government and the speaker.

I don't get it. You would have thought that question time and all parliamentary sessions would be compulsory for all members to attend. Will some politicians get docked pay for absenteeism? Do they need a medical certificate? Perhaps there should be a co-payment required by them for their salary for non-attendance.

Do people realise that the co-payment of $7 allows the government to actually reduce the amount of money paid to doctors and health care in general. They get a windfall from the public to put in their medical futures fund. Doctors get an extra $2 but the government has reduced their Medicare contribution by $7. Doctors who don't bulk bill will just put up their fees even more to cover any shortfall. Those budget bean counters are really clever! Or will be seen to be until some of them get sick and that may cause them to have a rethink. Someone should ask Minister Dutton if the government is paying less in Medicare refunds because of the co-payment. And also, whether any other Health money that had been targeted for research prior to this budget will continue.

Will there be a government MP given marching orders today just to prove yesterday wasn't an anomaly and to show that the Speaker is trying to be impartial?

I've been aware for a while that we have Question Time in Parliament. But I am yet to see an Answer Time where those questions are actually answered. Am I missing something?

Does the "and" count in a three-word slogan? I mean "debt AND deficit disaster" is four words. If the AND does count then the Coalition have shown that inflation is on the increase.

Who would you pick for the Supercoach team of politicians to lead the government and who would be Captain?

So, does George Brandis discriminate between the discrimination commissioners? Someone should report him! But to whom?

How things change over time. Hockey a radical student protesting about fees. Turnbull a former member of the Labour party. And look what fortune and fame have got them. Joe holds the purse strings of the nation. Malcolm holds...... Malcolm holds..... Oh well, if he had stayed with Labor, he would have been the longest serving PM behind Menzies and Howard. Still fortune and fame is everything.

Sadly, our governmental system remains locked in the past and the politicians cling on to the belief that they are the cream that has risen to the top instead of what some of them are - the things that rise to the top when the sewer backs up.

However, the issue is that our governmental system is at fault. Why do we need three tiers of government? Why do we have what is a two-party system? Why don't we just get the best people for the job; not those into power games, notoriety and self-flagellation? Why are they only held to account every three to four years and then we are forced to judge them on broken promises and promises for the next term? Why are they driven by weekly polls and not is what is best for Australia? Why are they so divisive? The opposition doesn't hold the government to account as an auditor does, so they are basically unemployed for three to four years. They seem bored, trying to be spoilsports because they were the least liked. How much money is wasted in duplication of resources, paying off companies for support etc.? How much time is wasted dealing with trivial things because the important ones are put in the too hard basket?

If the CO2 does go up then the ensuing climate change means that Gippsland will be sub-tropical to tropical. Barramundi at Lakes Entrance!!! Actually, the ice caps will melt and Lakes Entrance will be in Warragul. I need to consider asking my landlord to put in more drainage.

"Abbott does believe in climate change. Like some latter-day Noah or Kevin Costner from Waterworld (not Disneyworld), he has got his cabinet makers building an ark (de Triumphe). He has already got one woman (Bishop) one goose (Joyce) one weasel (Pyne). He believes that an NBN only needs go to a node because everything will be underwater anyway. Roads can far easily be turned into canals (did I really put far canal in the one sentence?) that is why he wants to buy boats in Indonesia and destroy them so that there is only one true Arc of the Covenant. Apparently, he is going to smuggle Cardinal Pell aboard as the figurehead. He doesn't need a helms "man" as the ship has been designed to continue to the right. He has his red budgie smugglers as his flag and his blue tie as a headband to give him a more raffish look. That is the only clothing item he intends wearing so that he can make page 3 of the Murdoch Press..................."

All you cynics out there should be severely chastised. The "do nothing" state government has finally decided to do something. It has saved all the money it should have spent fulfilling last pre-election promises to splurge on some new projects that may or may not be completed if it is elected. What a waste of our money. Governments build up a nest egg over three and a half years so that major things can appear to happen just prior to election. How gullible are we? We seem to elect parties of either persuasion who do the same thing each time they are elected, so the answer is very gullible.

The Abbott led government is tightening the purse strings. They are increasing petrol costs, targeting pensioners, cutting funding to public transport, charging students more, putting up medical costs and a range of other things. Don't they realise that it is an election year?............. Oh, they have three and a half more years. Oh, it is the State government that is in election mode. They are spending big on roads, rail, schools, aged care, hospitals......... Does anyone else notice this strange link between spending and election timing? Or is it just a strange coincidence?

Imagine a group of protagonists trying to achieve consensus in a schoolyard situation. One a mild-mannered thug who wants to throw his weight around; one a hard mouthed would be dictator; and the other a whining mummy's boy who twists truths to get his own way. On a completely separate matter any legislation that Tony Abbott wants passed is dependent on the triumvirate of Clive Palmer, Eric Abetz and Christopher Pyne achieving consensus.

Why is it that we seem to have our most venerated and respected members of our society selected to be our Governor General and not as our PM? Is it because the PM must come from a safe seat and therefore is only elected by a small select group to be a choice for PM?

If they were of the ilk of the last crop of our Governors General, we might respect them as leaders a whole lot more.

To the tune of Love and Other Bruises by Air Supply on the issue of the child abuse and the church

As George Pell starts pointing fingers
He's acting far too slow
Better if he practises what he preaches
And tells us what he knows
Now he denies the real truth
Even faced with gospel truth
Thugs and other bruisers and child sex abusers
And other pedophiles crushing children's smiles
Thugs and other bruisers and child sex abusers
Are devils in disguise, hiding behind the churches' lies
Orphans without a home

Were trapped and all alone
There was nothing they could do
But deal with it on their own
Now he denies the real truth
Even faced with gospel truth

People have generally maligned Matthew Guy's ability to plan for the future for Victoria. Surely his open slather approach to the building of high-rise structures is to be commended. This predicting of the rise in sea-levels due to the Federal Government's backward thinking about the environment, shows enormous insight.

The almighty America wants us to join another war and we unthinkingly tug our forelock, doff our cap and put on a soldiers' helmet. At the same time, we have been told that we have a higher chance of terrorism here in Australia and may need to consider bigger fridge magnets. We never made it to Rwanda, Eritrea and other war-torn zones which practised more horrific crimes against humanity because they had no oil. We should be alarmed at what this government is doing to us and be alert to the dangers they have placed our country in.

June

- **The military intervention against ISIL/ISIS begins**

Clive Palmer's wealth has reported dropped by a billion. How much will it increase with no carbon tax? Vested interested? Has he declared this?

Thank heavens that Labour is going to oppose these retrograde, divisive measures in the bills. If they didn't do that, then what would they have really stood for? Next steps are the on-shore processing of asylum seekers here in Australia and some positive steps on climate change. Labour needs to seek the higher ground lest climate change and global warming policies of Abbott catch them out of their depth.

Typical of repressed Christopher Pyne not allowing natural debating en masse

Add Assange and Hicks to political witch hunts where judiciary and legislature are too intertwined. At least here in Australia there is a nominal separation of powers

Turnbull is looking as being by far the best option as leader of this country. How does Tony keep his job or is workplace bullying allowed in the Liberal Party room?

Tony Abbott will argue that even such venerable Mexican scientists as El Nino and La Nina are poles apart on climate change so why should he believe in climate change.

How many light bulbs on the hill need changing? We normally associate light bulbs with innovation and new ideas. However, with this migration back to the Dark Ages no-one is burning the candle at both ends. Get a Science portfolio, some new and dedicated people in parliament instead of these energy saving globular types content to shed no light on what future Australia will look like.

There is so much tripe said in question time it turns one's stomach.

Politicians have mastered the art of faking sincerity. But the public want to know if there is a cure for gullibility and why the gullible pandemic occurs just prior to elections. Is it available on the PBS? Perhaps that is what the $5 co-payment for medical research should target first.

I think there should be a translation service provided for the public to listen to question time. There is so much polispeak, gibberish and gobbledygook spoken that it seems so much like Double Dutch. Well it is all Greek to me.

Given the numbers of people in both state and federal parliament perhaps there should be a cut in those. This would reduce the number of nodders behind ministers and shadow ministers during photo ops. Perhaps journalists should bypass the minister and ask a question of a nodder behind and see if they actually were listening or merely trying to stay awake.

How many politicians does it take to change a light bulb? You could ask the Science Minister if we had one; but the answer from the coalition would be "What are light bulbs? We use candles here in the Dark Ages where there is no global warming."

Even in sub-zero temperatures, the hot air that rises off cow manure and permeates Canberra saves on heating bills.

Good to see that politicians are doing their best for the environment. Both sides are recycling old arguments, re-using tried and failed policies and reducing any interest by the public!

It seems that Tony and his coalition may be relying on their "tax appeal" to win the hearts of voters.

Scott Morrison has informed Australians that some people who fled violence and danger in their own country, made it to Australia and then were subsequently exported to Manus Island and Nauru have now been found to be genuine refugees. He also stated that

they must earn their keep in Nauru or New Guinea or soon perhaps Cambodia. Australian's may abhor people smugglers but we now too have become them and worse still we have become slave traders. What price hypocrisy?

What do you call a child born in Australia? "Unlawful maritime arrival" according to the Immigration Department. The child's parents have journeyed to Australia fleeing persecution in their own country and even their child has been given an offensive label. Has the immigration department thought of tattoos on the child's wrist or yellow stars on their nappies to indicate they are inferior? They have been transferred to Christmas Island for medical reasons. Maybe that will be the only Christmas these kids will see in Australia.

Tony's moral compass will remain even more all over the shop once the poles melt. But head in the sand (at Bondi) he still won't see what he has created. Break out the floaties everyone. Canada you can understand wanting global warming but not us.

Religions promise immortality but somehow immorality seems to be part of the path to righteousness.

What many people realise is that in Australia the most common dress worn by Muslim women who practice traditional Islam is the Hijab. The Burqa as such is very rare. Banning the Burqa would do little except exacerbate the cultural divide and give extremists more ammunition to throw at westerners. If the Hijab is to be banned, do we then ban the habits worn by nuns? The culture that is associated with these types of dress is based on the perceived need for modesty. It has been interpreted as subjugation and perhaps in some family relationships subjugation is involved but there is no doubt that subjugation takes place in many forms in all cultures including western cultures. Why are there no female Catholic priests? Why can't priests marry so they can suffer like the rest of us?

When burqa, terrorist, ISIL and Iraq and Syria become the buzz words and make the front page, funny how the budget deficit, the Medicare co-payment, global warming, university fees and asylum seekers mental and physical health disappear off the radar. How many things will be allowed to slip through without parliament or public scrutiny because there is "an international humanitarian mission front" and centre. Good to see Essendon hasn't moved off the back pages though. It adds some sense of normality to life. I bet Denis Napthine would like a "war" to erupt involving Victoria at the moment to make the East-West tunnel, paramedics pay issues and many other hot issues disappear for a couple of months.

July

- **2,100 Palestinians and 71 Israelis are killed in fighting.**
- **Malaysia Airlines Flight 17, crashes in eastern Ukraine after being shot down by a missile. All 298 people on board are killed**
- **Clean Energy Legislation Bill passed, removing what was known as the carbon tax**

The Abbott Government isn't used to negotiating to achieve a consensus. It believes "mandate" means "consensus". See what happens when bullies are stood up to......... they just don't like it.

Why does it take years for asylum seekers who land in Australia to be processed and yet hours if at sea? Surely the speed of processing is the issue that needs to be dealt with. Instead of paying millions for sub-standard accommodation spend millions to improve the speed of processing and then give people asylum or send them home based on due and proper diligence in processing.

Senators need to vote on bills based on merit not on some preconceived notion that the government has that they must pass.

If we put wind farms on the floor of both chambers, the windbags there would drive them to ensure endless supply of power for Australia.

What we need is a Bronwyn Bishop in the chair as president of the Senate, then watch the number of non-liberal national party senators sent out before votes are taken. She sure knows how to run a house.

When we return asylum seekers who fear persecution back to the country they have fled from; what follow-up by the Australian government occurs to ensure that such persecution doesn't recur? Or is it a case of a quick check, a quicker handover and they become someone else's problem. If the German Jews had fled Germany in

the 1930's and arrived on our doorstep would we have handed them back the way we are treating the Tamils and others?

If the Australian Navy intercepted a boat of asylum seekers and then bailed them up and handed them over to another navy surely that is piracy. If they did the same in Australian waters then screened them briefly and then handed them over to another navy then surely that is lunacy. It would be in contravention to our commitment to the United Nations charter on refugees. If some Australian citizens were treated the same way on the open seas, all Australians would be livid. This government's policy on refugees makes you feel ashamed to be an Australian.

I wonder whether Morrison and Bishop are cosying up to Abe so they can send asylum seekers to Japan!

The headline questioned "Is this Murdoch's boldest move yet?" and the answer is a definite no. His boldest move was the far cheaper outlay to buy the influence over the current Australian Government. The cost was minimal as it only required a favourable editorial stance from his media outlets and the occasional dinner with Tony. One wonders when he will be given his wish to control all media in Australia. Has to be soon whilst Tony is still in power and the Pandora's box is in his hands. Now the carbon tax has gone bring on the media battle.

Abbott's quote "We are a conservationist government" shows a slip of the tongue. he was thinking "We are a conversationist government" We talk a lot about doing something to prevent global warming but actually won't do anything. It is all talk and no (direct) action.

So, the East West Freeway will cause the demolition of the just opened brand new 8-million-dollar facility for the training of guide dogs. I am sure Vision Australia, like the rest of Victoria at the last election, didn't see that coming.

Tony Abbott at the last election vowed to expedite the processing of refugees/asylum seekers by transferring them

off-shore to Manus Island and Nauru. It was called Fast Track Assessment and Removal Process. What has happened is that asylum seekers have been removed, but no processing has been completed in 5 months. Instead the New Guinea PM has decreed that a good majority are not genuine refugees. One wonders what the PM stands for after Tony Abbott's name. Poor Misguided? Puppet Master? Powerful Machiavellian? He has used the out of sight/out of the news policy effectively, so is Political Mastermind a worthy title? Somehow, I think Philanthropic (hu)Manitarian doesn't fit the bill.

We are incarcerating overseas people who have come to Australia in inhumane living facilities. If we were at war with their country, and they had been soldiers they would be treated better. If they were Australians who had murdered or raped, they would be treated better. Instead they are held without being assessed, without being charged for a crime, without having the opportunity to defend themselves in a court of law, appeal through the law courts and yet have been given an indefinite sentence. It is not against International or Australian law to seek asylum. We have laws that incorporate habeas corpus yet such laws don't apply to immigrants seeking asylum. If they are found to be economic refugees then we should create a law and charge them and if necessary, deport them. Perhaps such a law and the swift processing of that law would be a better deterrent than orange lifeboats, or concentration camp facilities and a Sergeant Schultz like government who bleat "I know nothing........... nothing"

We treat those in the juvenile justice system and in particular indigenous people only a little better. They are our own "economic refugees". We are so far behind the rest of the world in the treatment of indigenous people. In a first world country we have a third world group of people that we for too long have turned a blind eye towards. The latest repeal proposal of discrimination laws may satisfy the likes of

Andrew Bolt and other people with sunburnt necks but does little to endear us to any ethnic and indigenous group.

We need to clean up our own backyard before preaching to the world about human rights. Part of that is creating a society that has a social conscience where indigenous people are accepted and respected, where their dignity is allowed to remain intact and where they are supported as they need. However, that does not mean we should blindly and blithely accept how we treat those who seek asylum here. Justice should apply to all.

It seems that we are back on war footing again as we are about to be invaded. The government's covert operation is underway and due to operational matters at sea we will be unable to find out about the 153 Tamil asylum seekers from India who are about to invade our poor defenceless country. Or should that be "poor defenceless asylum seekers whose boat is to be invaded by our country"?

It is really Orwellian, this Animal Farm we have in Canberra called Parliament. So many turkeys ducking for cover as attack dogs try to ruffle a few feathers. They chicken out when it comes to positive policy making and are herded into the party room pens and come out sheepishly bleating the same dogma. So much horse trading goes on; along with catcalling and caterwauling that echoes across the chamber trying to make the other side look a goose. But they dress it up in business suits and if it wasn't for public seeing snouts in the trough and the bullshit around, it might be seen as civilised.

Congratulations to the State Government for sticking to their guns and delivering on the East-West tunnel. What a wonderful windfall for private enterprise. $2 billion to build a little bit of it. $1 billion to not build it. We now find out that the business case has nothing to do with value for money, it is more like money for nothing. The Victorian public gets screwed either way. At the next election we will just find out if it is a left-hand or right-hand thread.

When we got the Liberal/National Coalition to represent us, we wanted the promised public transport upgrades. Now we have the widening of the Tulla and the signing of the East-West Link. It's as if the Napthine Government is suddenly signing all these pre-nup agreements just before the November wedding day without consulting us?

Some treasurers see money as a tool.

Others are just tools with money.

The taxation system has enormous number of loopholes as has been evidenced by the offshoring of huge profits. What is needed are politicians who will stand up to companies who do these things and make sure that these manipulations are outlawed. Otherwise everyone has to pay more tax or we get less services. There is more scope for those higher income earners rather than PAYE taxpayers to manipulate their income tax but again we need politicians who are willing to close loopholes. Companies will try to maximise profits and pay less tax if they can; just as individuals will try to avoid tax if they can. Morality doesn't enter into it sadly. A moral and ethical company will not stay in business long if it has competition from a somewhat less moral but legally legit company. It says a lot about the morality of the politicians more than anything.

If history has taught us anything, it is that there is no such thing as a happy equilibrium in politics. When one political party gets in power there is a severe swing to that side and when they go too far, they are ousted and the swing goes too far the other way. It happened when Gough came to power and the electorate couldn't handle the dramatic and much needed swing. And when that swing went too far or was found to be unaffordable the "now small "l" liberal Malcolm Fraser went too far right, then Hawke/Keating got it pretty close to centre only to lose out to Howard................ and so on.

August

- The US begins an air campaign in northern Iraq to stem the influx of ISIS militants

It is about time that the media accepted some responsibility and perhaps some blame for the contempt that politicians seem to serve up to their constituents. Facile and fatuous sound-bites from doorstep interviews have become the basis for opinion pieces on television, radio, the internet and in print. When did fact checking and research go out of the journalistic kitbag? The general population has learned to expect that politicians have difficulty with the truth but it seems that the media, caught up in the frenzy of being first, are also losing a lot of credibility. Investigative journalism, pinning politicians down to answer questions, and presenting in-depth analysis once were the backbone of political journalists. Reporters are a thing of the past and now we have political commentators and instant deadlines. How can we as electors get a true picture when the politicians put out their spin to journalists who happily accept it or who just spin it a bit more? Policies and costings for every political party's platform should be demanded by the press and then properly scrutinised and truthfully reported by journalists. If journalists and editors went back to basics, the freedom of the press would mean something. It would mean that electors would be free to choose the government they want, knowing exactly what it was intending to do.

The founders of Canberra as Australia's seat of government have been proven correct. "Who in their right minds would go there?" Out in the middle of nowhere, it is a Bizarro world where refugees from normality seek asylum. Indeed, it is an asylum but with all the perks.

There is only one game in town and scoring points and winners are lauded. In the real, non-Bizarro world, the electors are the losers and can't see the point of it all. The political editors want to talk about "runs on the board" but sub-editors intervene and all we get are "puns for the bored". As a game you'd expect a sports report but all we get is a rorts report. We quite aptly appoint an opposition in this opposite place, whose job they describe as bringing the government down with reasonable debate yet in other countries this would be seen as treasonable negate.

Politicians' pork barrelling and having their snouts in the trough is an oxymoron. Though it seems that deprivation of oxygen is an issue; as the glasshouse effect of Canberra is a known cause of global warming. There is too much hot air and halitosis caused by the release of cattle excreta. Yet these people seek immortality and to be remembered whilst they question others' immorality as those lives are dismembered. There is more innuendo and smear than a proctologist would see in a lifetime's work.

Should we pay them more? Another "k" would turn money into monkey. We miss the fundamental principle of government though. Is it to have important decisions removed from our plate and debated by the best of our thinkers; or is it to imprison these primates who go around wearing blinkers?

In a true Bizarro world, Canberra would be known as Arrebnac, but it isn't. It can only be seen as that when you look in the rear-view mirror as you quickly leave. Canberra quite appropriately is located in a depression. Etymologists believe Arrebnac is a native word for "cloud cuckoo land." All I know is that as you enter Canberra you are asked to leave your sanity behind and there is an upper IQ level that prohibits anyone with three digits entering.

Ideally what Australians have under their electoral system is a team of people who elect a leader whom they think will best implement the policies of their party. These policies normally are outlined prior to the election and voters decide who in their electorate will best represent their viewpoint. Sadly, many

politicians put their party ahead of their electorate. Once they get their seat, they stand for nothing. And they may pay a price for that at the next election. Occasionally a Prime Minister will put him/herself ahead of their country and their party and too may pay a price.

"The Napthine government has little understanding about the need for public housing but is happy to meet the greed of property developers. The latest instalment of the lack of compassion is the money grab from those who can least afford it - the raising of rent for public housing tenants. The reason that the Napthine government give is that the Federal Government has given more money directly to people to offset any issues with the carbon tax. That is a spurious link at best. The real reason is that as landlords, they can. The same reason applies to the selling off of public housing sites and public land to the private developers. Next we will be expected to believe that the East-West road tunnel is part of the underground sequestration of carbon dioxide.

Many voters believe that the hearts of politicians are excised when they are elected but the saddest thing is that politicians think that the brains of voters are excised as they enter the polling booth."

There is a lot of pork barrelling of marginal electorates at the expense of much needed services in safe seats. Do both of the main political parties assume that we are stupid? Both are asking us to trust them. What is the past evidence we can base the allocation of our trust? They announce policies but the costings aren't available. Currently the Greens have thirty-nine requests for costings from the Departments of Treasury and Finance, Labour has five and the Coalition has none. Simple policies take two business days for costings to be done and more complex ones take five business days to be done. The two main parties must get their act together and submit requests for costings by the end of this week or the public and the media won't be given adequate time to assess them. If that

happens, they are treating electors with contempt and the whole process as a game or a joke. The bullying, snide remarks, lies and spin that they display is unworthy of them being in office at all. If they want the trust and respect of the electorate, they had better start earning it.

The biggest issue is actually politicians trying to make a "point of difference" between two similar policies. Just because one side says it is wrong the other side has to say it is right. Stupid system of government. Debates shouldn't always end with people agreeing to disagree. Don't you agree? This combative approach to politics is like the Game of Thrones without the sex, violence, passion and courage. doesn't hold our attention so we let it pass over. Bring back the old days where leaders of the tribes did all the fighting and at least we get to watch a decent spectacle.

Borders are artificial constructs yet are the cause of most of the world's conflict. Groups of people who are treated fairly within a country will want to remain in that country. Groups treated unfairly and forced to remain in that country will revolt or seek refuge elsewhere. Yet we criticise these people and blame the victims in such places as the Ukraine, Gaza, Afghanistan, Syria and Sri Lanka to name a few. It has been the same throughout history where brute force is used to keep the peace. We need to create societies throughout the world where people want to stay and that way there is more chance of peace.

Education reform seems to be off the government's agenda, yet reform needs to happen in the government's own education. For example, cutting taxes such as mining and carbon will not increase revenue. A life lost in a plane crash or a car crash is just as tragic. Kidnapping people on the high seas is piracy no matter how you spin it. A child's death in Gaza, Israel or Somalia are all equally a waste. Saying there is no such thing as global warming doesn't make it so. Arrogance and condescension aren't usually seen as virtues in leadership.

Egalitarian education and elitist education systems don't provide the same outcomes for everyone. Governments learn far quicker when they are thrown out of office. When will we get government education reforms?

The rich versus poor is the wrong debate. What is more important is the one about opportunity and who gets it and who is deprived of it. Education has always been the best way to expand the opportunities for all individuals, yet this government in dismissing most of the Gonski reforms, has effectively shut the door on opportunities for many Australians, who also happen to fall in the "poor" category. This allows these people to be kept in their place and Australia is the poorer for it. As a land of opportunity supposedly, Australia needs to foster the intellectual growth of all its citizens and thus equip them with options when the economy turns sour. Yet without radical change in the funding arrangements for schools and universities that gives everyone a real chance, we are effectively stunting that intellectual growth that will make Australia more prosperous. We are creating through the current selective funding of education, the Aussie version of the society of Aldous Huxley's "Brave New World".

Remember the way it used to be. To get a building permit you applied to council, who would then agree or disagree. If there were still any objections or the local council refused, then it could be taken before an independent umpire, VCAT and a decision was made. If there were still objections the final recourse was the Minister for Planning. Nowadays there seems to be no local government input, no need for an independent umpire, developers in Melbourne bypass all these checks and balances and red tape and go straight to the Minister for a final decision, usually yes. IBAC has no teeth and the Auditor General reports after the fact so we know that at least one Ministerial Department is always open for business.

The solution of withholding any aid money and starving people in poorer countries to death could work except that weight of numbers would see us as easy pickings. The ruling classes in France tried to starve the poor population and what was the result? Someone made a fortune spruiking Les Mis all around the world! So you would have them eating cake? Unless it is a Magic Pudding, you can't have your cake and eat it too. If countries ensure their citizens have basic human rights, are fed, clothed, have good health and have gainful use of their time, then there is less chance of any revolution. History has taught us that, but we haven't learnt yet. If China and India really flexed their economic muscle then Australia would become a third world country quite quickly. And we would have the issue of starving to death. We align ourselves with the US to try to stop that happening except the US is now heavily in debt to the Chinese. Perhaps we should cut out the middle man and drop the US and cosy up to China and India even more. We have lots of yellow cake that they think looks quite yummy.

As they pride themselves as economic managers, the coalition in both State and Federal arenas should be aware of the concept of "substance over form". Yet what we are finding is that there is a shroud of secrecy that envelops these governments. Accountability seems to be bypassed because of "commercial in confidence" and "national security operations". Taxes are raised to be spent by governments on our behalf so in essence that makes us shareholders and the government the Board of Directors. How many of us would like to sack the Board because of incompetence? Has ASIC started an investigation yet?

September

- Australia raises its terror threat level to high because of militants returning from ISIS battles in the Middle East.
- The United States and several Arab partners begin their airstrike campaign in Syria.
- Australia sends some combat aircraft and special forces to the Middle East to fight against ISIS
- Major raids in Australia on suspected terrorists
- In a referendum, Scotland votes against independence from the United Kingdom
- Hong Kong's government headquarters is occupied by thousands of protesters. Hong Kong police resort to tear gas to disperse protesters but thousands remain.
- Police carry out the nation's biggest ever counter-terrorism raids, with 15 arrests in Sydney and Brisbane, sparked by intelligence reports that Islamic extremists were planning random killings.

Very few people are in the chamber on the government side when Bill Shorten is speaking? Have the non-attendees refused to work without a good excuse and still receive government support?

Is question time just a photo op for non-attendees during normal sitting time? Please nod if the answer is yes.

There should be declarations by politicians of interest not just pecuniary, but actual interest in legislation. It looks like many politicians should sign the register of disinterest that most Australians have signed already. We elected the people who sit in the Houses of Parliament..... and we should be ashamed.

John Madigan should step aside as he doesn't belong in politics. Morality, ethics and principles are not wanted and of little use in parliament. Bring in someone else that we can rely on not to tell the truth and we'll all feel better then

When is a commitment, a promise or a blood oath or dead, buried and cremated?

When the west invaded Iraq and toppled Saddam they offered a western style democracy to a group of people who had no experience of it and who found that there were no real benefits as their lives were suddenly harsher. Of course, they turned to leaders who promised more. If the western nations had offered democracy and economic stability the situation would have been much better.

Cuba was no accident. Castro offered hope when there was none. Mao offered hope, Lenin offered hope, Hitler offered hope. They rose to power when the divide between rich and poor, aided and abetted by the wealthy and religious leaders, caused too much for the masses to bear.

So what does Tony offer? Not hope just hype!

Christopher Pyne needs to lift his game. The education standards in this country must be falling. Look who we think are the best people to represent us.

Abbott is also ahead of Bill Shorten in the "better PM" stakes, 41 per cent to 37 per cent. 22 per cent of those polled are uncommitted. Does that mean that the 78% are committed and if so to which asylum?

Who marks attendance at Parliament? Can politicians be docked pay for not turning up when parliament is sitting? And if they don't turn up why are they not on a six-month exclusion for actually being unemployed?

If there can be screens made available for people in the gallery to view information; can they not also have a Brownlow Medal like Tally board that shows the number of politicians ejected from the house and which team they play for?

I hear that the odds of a coalition member being thrown out are now at 200-1. But given the pictures of the senate, it looks like

the president has thrown out nearly everyone there. So Bronnie Bishop, lift your game!!!

Can we just please have reruns of the ABC's program Utopia played instead of Question Time. That way we will see how governments work without the dull boring bits.

Do politicians wear ties or pearls so that you can't see the circumcision marks on their necks?

"Having seen the living conditions on Manus Island via TV, I wonder whether many of the prisoners in our gaols convicted of crimes, some heinous, would gladly swap their hotel like accommodation for the unconvicted asylum seeker accommodation that our generous government thinks is humane?"

I feel sorry for the civilian Palestinians who are caught up in this battle of historical proportions. The myth is that their land is being encroached by Israelis is no myth. In 1948 they were kicked out of an area of land they had lived in for centuries so that Israel could be established, an area that they had previously shared with Jews and other religious groups over a long period of time. That decision by the UN though appearing correct to the western world at the time has had dreadful consequences ever since. To the Palestinians it would be like asking the US to make New York the new home of the Jews or Greater London for the British. Arbitrary borders have ruined people's lives for years and the carving up of Africa and the Middle East by European colonisation regardless of cultural and ethnic backgrounds of inhabitants has been the bugbear of second and third world countries. Now exploitation takes place by multinationals backed by government rather than countries on their own. the people who are caught up in this and bear the brunt of exploitation and armed conflict are Joe Hockey's leaners and Scott Morrison's economic refugees.

But what do many western civilised society people care? A plane load of passengers in a jet lose their lives and all hell breaks loose. All hell breaks loose in Gaza and thousands of lives are lost and it just makes the news. If it happened in Africa or South America it wouldn't even make the news. What value do we put on a single human life? Or is that dependent on what the colour of your skin is, your cultural or religious background, the country you live in and your wealth or lack of it?

I am pissed off with the world and its lack of humanity at the moment

We need to hold our elected representatives, of whichever persuasion, accountable. We need to demand of them honesty, integrity and a sense of responsibility to only offer what they can and will deliver. Until we do that, we will always have the situation where "honest politician" is an oxymoron.

Overheard in Cabinet. "Hey Scott, I'm stuck on 9 Down. It says 'asylum seeker' and it is two words. The first is 7 letters and the second is 7 letters too."

"That's 'illegal arrival'"

"I tried it Scott, but the only thing that does fit is 'anxious refugee'"

"You must have made a mistake somewhere else"

"Oh yes, I did. You told me to put 'humanitarian' for 2 across a word meaning Immigration Minister, when it should have been 'totalitarian'"

In looking back over the election promises of successful candidates over the past twenty years, there has been a clear pattern of linguistics used. It is a mixture of spin, deceit and obfuscation. Some examples are:

"Will" means "might"

"Promise" and "guarantee" have the rider "void after the forthcoming election"

"By the end of the second term of office" translates as "never" or "we hope you will have forgotten by then"

"We are considering this" refers to "We haven't even thought about this"

"I'm glad you brought this to my attention" can be decoded as "I thought that was dead and buried"

"There is an enormous black hole left by our opponents" really means "We have a get out of gaol clause when we need it"

"That will be the first thing on my agenda" translates as "There are so many 'first things' that I have lost count"

"Our opponents achieved nothing in their last term of office" has the fine print "And we will follow suit"

"I will represent all of my electorate not just those who voted for me" can be interpreted as "I will follow the party line even if it runs at cross purposes to my constituents"

"It is a great honour and privilege to be your elected member" can be unspun to reflect "I won't have to canvass your opinion and your vote for another four years."

Let's hope that whoever gets elected in the next election speaks openly, honestly and without spin.

When dealing with weighty matters such as: global warming issues, tax havens for multinationals, asylum seeker assistance, trade deals, ebola, peace in the Middle East etc.; the current government has two distinct operating procedures. On the home-front, it is confected outrage. On the world stage, it is defective courage.

<u>October</u>

- Once in a century rainfall hits Sydney.
- Joko Widodo was inaugurated as the 7th President of Indonesia
- Tony Abbott threatens to "shirtfront" Vladimir Putin over the downing of a plane in the Ukraine.

Free foot check for politicians. I wonder how many politicians will be assessed as down at heel, the poor old soles.

I think blue ties should be banned from parliament as the people wearing them are masquerading as kind, caring people with social consciences.

Global warming's source has been found. It is in the houses of Parliament in Canberra. A mix of hot air fuelled by cattle excreta is generating enormous energy yet nothing gets done. All the energy dissipates into thin ozone depleted air and is not plugged into any grid to be of any benefit to the Australian Public. That is why we have to rely on coal generated power. If we could just harness all that wasted energy in Canberra.....

In a desperate bid to increase revenue, a tax on air has been discussed. As there are many more poor people than rich, it will fit into the Liberal Party's ideology. A co-payment system will be introduced and for those who can't afford it..... well let's say there will be fewer leaners than lifters in the future. Will this pass the Senate, a chamber well known for its hot air? Well don't hold your breath.... or perhaps you should, just in case!

The RET has helped Napthine in his electorate. Hundreds unemployed there because he doesn't like wind farms and the renewable energy sector there has collapsed, the highest youth unemployment in the state, and local retail and businesses closing

rapidly. The Coalition may win in November but he could easily not be in Parliament himself.

If Tony Abbott has to eat humble pie about going back on the election promise regarding the GST will there be any GST on the pie? Is it cooked or uncooked?

With Medibank Private to be sold off, will there be anything left for the next government to sell off to pay for their mismanagement?

So will Dennis Napthine, the Premier of Victoria be inviting his favourite Prime Minister to spruik on the election trail and thank him for the money to build the unwanted East west tunnel? I think not. Victorians won't be able to afford to buy petrol and use their cars and pay tolls to use the new white elephant tunnel. How appropriate that the tunnel is right next to the elephant enclosure at the zoo.

With Turnbull's revamped NBN no-one will be downloading stuff anyway. It will be on free to air TV quicker than pirating it.

Apparently one Nationals politician tried to download data from the Bureau of Meteorology about it being hotter 118 years ago to try to prove climate change isn't happening. He now wants an inquiry as to why that data doesn't exist. If we download stuff we can get "fined". He can't "find" stuff to download.

What is metadata? Is there a definition yet? I've downloaded a lot of different definitions about what it is. Will I be hauled before the courts for that downloading? Will I get gaoled for that?

George Christensen should take his problem about missing records to the Science Minister..... Oh, wait, he should then take his problem about the missing Science Minister to the Prime Minister who is missing in action in all the press releases today.

**"There will be another million cars on the road soon...........
not Holden or Ford of course but still the push is for more road infrastructure. I don't get it. Surely if you were advocating for more roads you should be supporting a car industry otherwise the profits**

go off shore. The cost for public transport infrastructure can't be as much as it is for road per person who uses it. And the running/fuel cost per person of driving a car compared to an electric train should be higher one would think. The greenhouse gas emissions would be lower for trains than cars, wouldn't they? With a bit of luck Geoff Shaw may lose the balance of power and things like the east-west tunnel will go.

What's next for Scott Morrison in his obsession to stigmatise and further traumatise asylum seekers? Perhaps a yellow star on their clothing as they head into their concentration camp detention? Would tattooed barcodes on their arms speed up their processing?

I'm just wondering if climate change will see the jobs for water diviners dry up......................"

Going back to medieval times, the first estate refers to the clergy, the second to the nobility, the third to the commoners. How little has changed even here in the so-called egalitarian society within Australia. The clergy appears to be above the law. The nobility is based on wealth often passed down from one generation to another. The commoners are being kept in their place by ever dwindling entitlements. Our noble families such as the Packers, Murdochs and the Rineharts of this world wield power over the government and as more stories unfold, we will see more and more calling in of favours. As they also control the "fourth estate", the media, it is a two-pronged attack that any government struggles to survive. Reminds us of the idiom, "he who lives in Point Piper calls the tune."

As far as Israel and Palestine goes. That area has been fought over for so long that they build ruins on ruins on ruins. And if you look at the climate, the terrain and the abysmal geology, you must wonder why they have fought over it. Is it a case of people saying,

"I don't want it"

"Neither do I, you have it"

"I will fight you for the right not to live here."

George Brandis tried to explain the proposed collection of metadata. What a metadisaster!!

Our immigration policy is "out of sight, out of mind". Australians aren't being shown the human face of the refugees. We don't know their names. We aren't shown what sort of conditions they have fled from. The government knows that as soon as we see those things, outpourings of empathy and sympathy by Australians will occur. That is why they must be processed overseas. The uncaring government doesn't want us to care and they are having great success in doing just that. Faceless asylum seekers are given numbers, located and settled in places offshore that we wouldn't like to see our children grow up in. We stop short of how the Nazis dealt with Jews, Poles, homosexuals etc.; but only marginally short.

The injury list grows for Team Australia.

* Eric Abetz is having difficulty walking with his foot in his mouth.

* George Brandis too is needing a podiatrist after shooting himself in the lower extremity.

* Joe Hockey has tripped over some ill-timed words and bad statistical selections.

* Julie Bishop has starred recently staring down the opposition, but can't do it all on her own.

* Christopher Pyne, the snipey backpocket tagger, has gone quiet

* David Johnson in charge of the defence structure has gone MIA probably from jet lag

* Scott Morrison, the star centre half forward, has been isolated so many times in a game. Having not attended any training camp it looks like he may have missed the boat this time around

* The usually industrious Ian McFarlane has been constantly bypassed and has nothing to do

* Greg Hunt, once the crowd favourite is still stuck on the (left) wing and getting little encouragement from his team-mates

However, the captain coach, Tony Abbott, will soon be told that he has the full support of the board (IPA and Rupert Murdoch) and then he'll know his job is in doubt.

Meanwhile former captain coach Malcolm Turnbull sits on the pine week after week wearing the green vest, unable to get a run and starved of opportunities.

November

- **Jacqui Lambie threatens to vote down every piece of Government legislation until the Federal Government improves a pay rise for defence force personnel.**
- **The Intergovernmental Panel on Climate Change (IPCC) releases the final part of its Fifth Assessment Report, warning that the world faces "severe, pervasive and irreversible" damage from global emissions of CO_2**
- **Bronwyn Bishop takes a $5000 helicopter flight to attend a Liberal Party function. This would ultimately end her position as Speaker of the House.**
- **G20 Summit held in Brisbane where Tony Abbott had said he was going to 'shirtfront' Vladimir Putin**

Doorstops, pressers, announcements, cash splurges, tweets, instagrams.... what ever happened to detailed information about policies and how they will be funded. Do we have to decide on a candidate on photoshopped photopped charisma?

Why did the Premier ignore the advice of his most senior transport planners and opt for the less cost effective east West Tunnel over Melbourne Metro and then keep all the details a secret?

What promises will each party actually keep? Which party will actually be honest?

Pay TV viewers may seek a refund for dud programming on the Vic election debate.

Perhaps the Defence Minister is looking for manufacturers who will make barbed wire vessels, ones to help him and his party traverse the creek they find themselves up.

With the major parties now looking at how the micro-political parties manipulate preferences and quotas, and how the names of parties are so similar to major parties; can we rename Clive Palmer's Party. It is his "pet" project so should it be called the PUP-PET party?

"With the government's response to climate change being a head in the sand approach, we may not know where the "tropics" may mean Tasmania. Apparently, the government won't start doing anything about it come hell or high water............... I wonder which one they will acknowledge first?"

Global warming is not caused by carbon dioxide in the atmosphere though. It is caused by all the daylight saved over the years. It must be stored underground because there are so many people with their head in the sand looking for it.

A rose by any other name would smell as sweet." Scott Morrison thinks that having his staff call asylum seekers, "illegals" and "detainees" rather than clients will somehow make everything all right and somehow permit genuine refugees to miss out on their international human rights. If that is the case, perhaps we should use appropriate words for our politicians such as "fraudsters", "corrupt", "bigoted", "xenophobic", "liars", "cheats", "morally bankrupt". Would that make it right? According to Scott Morrison's perception of the world it just might.

Based on religious and ethical grounds, euthanasia of the terminally ill who are begging to have their pain and suffering ended, is illegal. Most religions espouse the virtues of a moral and well lived life and the glories of heaven. It seems sadly ironic that these same groups force so many good and moral people to go through a living hell to get to a peaceful heaven.

Here's a novel idea to boost the chances of young Australians to get a home of their own and allow the empty apartments in cities to be tenanted. If the negative gearing tax incentive was removed, investors would look elsewhere perhaps into renewable energy development and many houses and apartments would come onto the market at an affordable price.

So, Scott Morrison is hell bent on punishing those who can't defend themselves despite their refugee status. "Australia will no longer resettle people found to be refugees by UNHCR in Indonesia" You have to wonder if Scott Morrison is actually human, because I can't see any trace of humanity!

No-one should have any doubts that we have a capitalist form of government in Australia. Unions and businesses can buy influence. At election times, parties use market forces to gain power. The community want hope and so parties sell it along with snake oil and smoke and mirrors. But you do have to wonder why Australia is in debt when one government department is making money hand over fist. Heaven help us if we privatise the Mint.

The issue is the system. We have inherited a feudal system but the architects of our constitution saw Australia as a Federation of States and that is why the Senate exists to protect state interests. They didn't perceive that we as a country would be so interlinked through advances in technology that the notion of states becomes a relic of the past that we cling to. We are over-governed and we only need a two-tiered government not three. Proportional representation and quota system used by upper houses is as archaic as the preferential system of voting but we cling to those because our constitution is sacrosanct. To change the constitution, we need a referendum that is effectively controlled by state and federal governments who rely on the status quo to survive.

Someone has just told me that Scott Morrison's humanity is about as real as Santa Claus. I am totally devastated!! At the age of 58, I have just learned there is no Santa Claus.

Refugees escape a living hell and try to get to a more heavenly Australia only to end up in purgatory in off shore detention centres. Just how many refugees have been processed in these out of sight out of your mind places?

Q: How long does it take to process a refugee?

A: How long is a piece of red tape?

How impressive is the new environment policy for the Federal Government? They believe that the rise in sea levels will provide valuable water to put out the unseasonal fires and also break the drought.

Religion and faith is not a science and therefore there is no right and wrong answer just lots of different ones and many of them clash and none have been proven. We are supposed to live in ecumenical and egalitarian times but we are so far from it. One person's truth is another person's lie. Everyone has a different moral and ethical compass yet we stereotype people to particular images.

Is the answer to have no religion at all? Yet atheism is a belief in itself. Some people need a belief system just to get through their day. Why should we destroy that belief? What do we gain from it? If it is not thrust down our throats and we have to convert; why can't we just let them be? We have laws to protect the weak and at times insulate the rich. If the billions of Moslems around the world were indeed hell bent on converting others could they be stopped? No! But they are not. The vast majority of Moslems aren't extremists. They are just normal human beings who believe in things slightly differently to those of other religions. If you read the Bible (old and new Testaments), the Quran, the Torah, the teachings of Buddha etc., there are many parts that state there is only one true religion, but also there are many things in common such as love, friendship, honour, respect and individual accountability that we have based our societies on. Just because I think that you are wrong in your beliefs doesn't mean that I can throw these important aspects out the window and vilify and denigrate you. I would not be doing that "in good faith".

Should we be allowed to challenge the belief systems of others? Of course; but what is the motive? How do we go about doing it? If these two questions can be justifiably answered and the challenge is within the law, then that is fine. If we want to bend or change the law (e.g.18c) so that we can do or say anything with impunity, then we have effectively disposed of an agreed social norm and there is no protection for the weak who must either put up with it or in all likelihood end up lashing out.

It all comes down to motive and method.

Should we be free to say or do anything to others just because we can? Is that the true freedom of speech that we have championed a right for? What people forget is that with every right goes a responsibility. You may be right that the earth is not flat but if you abuse, denigrate, humiliate, demean and disrespect me in the process, you will have more trouble convincing me and provoke a reaction that you might not expect. This is how a society works through awareness, understanding and respecting others. Extremists of all religions forget that. Luckily the majority of people on this planet are social rather than anti-social beings.

If Tony Abbott is concerned that the back bench are revolting then he should have a look at the opinion polls and his policies. They aren't looking too flash either

December

- Tony Abbott announces changes to the government's paid parental leave scheme
- The Federal Government announces that it will scrap over 200 government agencies.
- Foreign aid slashed by $3.7 billion
- Terrorist siege in Sydney leaving many injured, two innocent and the terrorist dead
- Tony Abbott backtracks on parts of the budget
- Royal commission investigating the former Labor government's home insulation scheme.

In response to a comment about Parliament being like an episode of Get Smart It would be better with Milton the Monster "and now for a touch of tenderness for without a touch of tenderness it might destroy me..... oops too much". Imagine Tony, Christopher, Scott, Joe and perhaps even Bronnie with some extra tenderness.

In response to Tanya Plibersek stating that the refugee problem in countries neighbouring Syria would be like a million people moving to Sydney If a million people moved to Sydney, perhaps they could all move into Scott Morrison's or Tony Abbott's electorate.

If Tony Abbott has done an about face on things, just how many faces does he have?

Anyone else notice the lack of seatbelts in the car carrying, Muir, Laundy and Scott? Is this an example of politicians putting their lives on the line? If so, perhaps they deserve the same pay increment that they are offering our defence force......... an effective pay cut.

Twas the last week of Parliament when all through the house not everyone was listening so the speaker did grouse

The PM was speaking and the opposition giving cheek so our dear Bronnie will break more records this week.

Those on her left will be withered by her stare as she tries to impose her rule from the chair.

Some will still mutter under their breath for it's Bron, not Julie's staring death.

Many will be asked to close the door on the way out but only those on the left without doubt.

As their numbers very swiftly and suddenly decline yet another mockery passed that we call question time.

It's Pyne and that C word all over again....... condescending!

Most of the main players in Parliament look like death warmed up, irradiated by Julie's death stare. The government seems to be comatose except for Scott Morrison who doesn't have a heart anyway. BS seems to have been stung by his own zingers and shows little life. Perhaps Bron, instead of sending people to the naughty corner should defrib the lot of these zombies.

At least there is some consolation. Next election Tony won't be able to say that he will stop the boats. With the coalition policy on climate change the ice caps will melt and we will all be in boats................ perhaps that's why he was looking to buy Indonesian fishing boats. Undercut the market! He's not a Rhodes scholar for nothing! His flying visits overseas are to check out possible high ground to escape to. With Gina and Clive making huge holes in the ground though, that should take up some of the excess water. Clive is already got his Titanic and I hear his dinosaurs can float.

Australians won't agree to switch Australia Day from the 26th of January which is the date that Europeans invaded. Though it would make more sense to have it on the anniversary of Federation, it would break with tradition. Federation took place on January 1st and the tradition is to seek more public holidays rather than less.

There is danger lying in wait in the speed in which the change in oil politics is happening. The US has been shipping arms to those countries that now are suddenly in decline. Part of the issue with terrorism and wars has been the inequality caused by capital. The US arms diplomacy it has practiced for years will come back and bite them in the bum. The planes, bombs and other weaponry may be targeted at the US and its new allies. Russia won't go down without a fight. Imagine what will happen when we get another gunslinger Republican president in the Whitehouse. Australians won't need life insurance so there goes another industry down the tube.

Sometimes I think that we should put all the politicians from all countries in the middle of a minefield and force them to walk their way out. At the moment oil and innovation are power. In a way I hope Australia doesn't get too far into these realms as then we become a target. So if anyone of you accidentally whilst digging in your garden finds a massive oil deposit, don't tell anyone.

The climate science is real and this rise in oil economics will just speed up the process. If only we could be innovative enough to find a way of powering cars and industry with CO2 to balance things out a bit.

With apologies to Walt Whitman and to Robin Williams in Dead Poet's Society.....

"O Captain! My Captain! What the hell have you done;
We can't defend every attack, caused by your miscreant tongue;
The election's near, the polls we fear, the backbench is revolting,
We fellow Libs surely feel, resigning would show you're caring"

If we keep tossing out Prime Ministers no-one will want the job. Would we be better off with no-one? Perhaps that is the solution. Elect a group of people who will all work together in the best interests of Australia. No parties, no leaders..... might be worth a go.

Tony Abbott wants to fight everyone. He wants to fight Labor. He wants to fight the Human Rights Commission. He wants to fight asylum seekers. He wants to fight anyone he thinks could be a terrorist. He took on Phil Ruddick and won. He beat the backbench. Why doesn't he take on the multinationals that pay very low taxes? Or would that be punching above his weight. Instead of the Fenech "I loves ya all"; he merely says, "I stopped the boats. I stopped the mining and carbon taxes." He is so busy fighting everyone that he has no time to lead, develop and implement policies that are fair for all Australians or is he going to fight us too? In the long run Bill Shorten could win the bout without laying a glove on Tony who may end up prone on the floor having accidentally knocked himself out.

Joe Hockey's proposal to "dip into your super" to buy a house is ludicrous at best. Joe is moaning about the cost to society of the "oldies" yet his advocated changes to super will see more needing a pension. People who accrue lots of super shouldn't need the pension. It is false economics and makes a mockery of the intergeneration report. Following his logic about opening up super where does it stop? I need a new car, a holiday, kids' private school fees, pay of HECS debt, pay GP co-payment bill?

When you are young and want to buy a house you have little or no super to dip into so what is the point of opening it up to housing? I can't believe that someone who proposes an idea like this is in charge of our economy. But then again, he thinks negative gearing is the way forward. He doesn't recognise an oxymoron when he sees it.

Governments of all persuasions make all sorts of dumb decisions supposedly on commercial principles and in the best interests of the public. Yet the reality is that they make decisions that may make them more popular at an election. In the case of funding transport, they don't care about how many bums on seats can be transported quickly at the lowest cost. The only bum they want on a seat is theirs in Parliament.

Tony Abbott is continuing to demonstrate that he is a sore loser over the East-West Link. He said that Victorians should treat the state election as a referendum on it, and he lost. He then said that money Victoria would have got would not be forthcoming, now we

are told that foreign investment will suffer and that the Andrews government is "abrogating people's rights". He again is showing that he thinks bullying is the answer to everything. Victoria voted against the Link so Tony please respect our "lifestyle choice".

Politicians when they are newly elected are optimistic and enthusiastic and seem to have a genuine desire to help all Australians. Is there something about Canberra, Parliament House, the party system or the "game of politics" that sucks the enthusiasm and optimism out of people? They then become merely a whole lot of faceless people out of touch with reality and mouthing words that they don't believe. Is this why young people are becoming reluctant to enter politics?

There is taunting across the playground as two gangs face off. Bullying is rife. Then someone calls the bullies bluff and they are shown to be cowards. Dummies are spat and vindictive threats are made but this is the way it has always been. However, it isn't at a kindergarten or school because it wouldn't be tolerated. It is happening daily in the Federal Parliament. Politicians expect respect and deference and we are stupid enough to give it to them and also let them get away with their immature antics. Doesn't say much for us does it?

The Australian Characters

Tony Abbott
    Anthony Albanese
    Cory Bernardi
    Bronwyn Bishop
    Julie Bishop
    George Brandis
    Michaelia Cash
    Mathias Cormann
    Peter Dutton
    Josh Frydenberg
    Julia Gillard
    Pauline Hanson
    Joe Hockey
    Barnaby Joyce
    Craig Kelly
    Jacqui Lambie
    Michael McCormack
    Scott Morrison
    Clive Palmer
    Christopher Pyne
    Kevin Rudd
    Bill Shorten
    Angus Taylor
    Malcolm Turnbull
    Penny Wong

Tony Abbott

Tony Abbott was a very divisive person who rose to Opposition leader after being a minister in an earlier Coalition government. He rose even higher to become Prime Minister. As Opposition leader he was masterful and opposed almost everything that the government put forward. He was also very divisive within his own party ousting Opposition leader Malcolm Turnbull who repaid the favour by ousting him after Abbott became PM. A member of the right wing, Tony Abbott opposed Marriage Equality and Climate Change, denying the later saying that it was 'crap'. He defended big business, refusing to call a Royal Commission into banking and saying that 'Coal was good for humanity'. One of his strangest decisions was to reinstall knighthoods and knight Prince Phillip. After losing the Prime Ministership, he moved to the backbench promising not to undermine and snipe, yet that is precisely what he did and assisted in ousting PM Turnbull. Eventually he was beaten in the 2019 election and his blue-ribbon Liberal seat became an independent one.

Anthony Albanese

A very popular member on the Labor side of politics, Anthony Albanese was narrowly defeated by Bill Shorten as he attempted to become Opposition Leader. After Bill Shorten's defeat in the 2019 election, he was elected Opposition leader. A normally quietly spoken person some believe that he does not have the strength to win an election.

Cory Bernardi

Cory Bernardi as a senator from South Australia for the Liberal Party helped swing the party even further to the right especially on such issues as marriage equality and acceptance of any gender issues including the teaching of sex education in schools. He made the statement that homosexual relationships were just a step away from having sex with animals. A strong fundamentalist Christian he was against abortion and railed against Islam and the immigration of Muslims into Australia and met with ultra-right-wing advocates from overseas. He believed that the ABC as a broadcaster should have its funding reviewed if it continued to express views other than his own. In 2017 just after winning his seat as a Liberal, he split from the Liberal Party to form his own Conservative Party. This party of one eventually failed and he returned to the Liberal fold before announcing his retirement from Parliament in 2020.

Bronwyn Bishop

As Speaker in the House of Representatives who is supposed to be unbiased when making rulings, Bronwyn Bishop ruled with an iron fist and that fist was always on her right hand. The left side, the non-Coalition one, took the brunt of the force she exuded in the position of power she held. She set a record for the number of people she ejected from the chamber. Her position became untenable however because she claimed travel expenses of $5000 for a private helicopter flight to travel 80km to a Liberal party function.

Julie Bishop

Julie Bishop held the deputy leader position for the Liberal government from the time it went into Opposition in 2007 and saw four male colleagues come and go as leader of the party. She was a Minister between 2003 and 2007 and again from 2013 to 2018 when she was Minister for Foreign Affairs. A forthright speaker, she was known for her 'death stare', fashion sense and rarely seen dry sense of humour.

George Brandis

Known as 'Bookshelf Brandis' because of the very large and expensive bookshelves he had installed in his parliamentary office to store all his legal books, George Brandis served as a minister in the dying days of the Howard Government in 2007. From 2013 to 2015 he was made Attorney-General and Minister for the Arts, during which time he cut $105 million from the arts budget. He was left out of the ministry in 2015 but became Leader of the Government in the Senate. He was given a retirement gift of the High Commissionership in London in 2017. He was hailed by all sides of politics for the speech he gave condemning Pauline Hanson's wearing of a burka in the Senate.

Michaelia Cash

Michaelia Cash has seemed out of her depth in whatever portfolios she has been involved in. Accident prone and lacking in the understanding of what her powers are, she has been involved I many gaffes and abuses of power. Prime Ministers have nt known where to hide her. In one case, her staffers did their best and shielded her from questions by the media with a whiteboard. She has beautifully coiffed hair that shows that she is ding her best to delete the ozone layer. As speaker she is very good for the deaf as her lip movements are exaggerated. George H Bush may have said "Read my lips", but with Michaelia Cash, her lips seem to work on their own.

Mathias Cormann

Mathias Cormann held many positions in government and in opposition. His Belgian accent made him sound like Arnold Schwarzenegger but his dry wit and intelligence easily surpassed anything Schwarzenegger had to offer. He was articulate as Leader of the Government in the Senate and often called upon to argue strongly in the public arena on money matters. He served time as Finance Minister and was caught out smoking cigars with Joe Hockey at the time of the budget from hell. When leadership spills occurred as Malcolm Turnbull jockeyed to keep his position, he misread the situation and changed sides which ultimately led to the ascension of Scott Morrison.

Peter Dutton

Unfortunately blessed with the face of a funeral director, Peter Dutton has wielded power in the immigration/home affairs portfolio with the same compassionless façade. His ministry's powers have grown as has his standing within the Liberal Party despite his often poor timed and poor choice of words. He challenged for the leadership against Malcolm Turnbull and on the second challenge felt confident he would win and become PM, only to be undercut by Scott Morrison. A member of the right wing of the government he still manages to steer the government away from a centralist course and often is accused of speaking too much outside his portfolio.

Josh Frydenberg

As a relatively young person Josh Frydenberg moved up the ladder quite quickly to the point where he became deputy leader of the Liberal party and the country's treasurer. His main claim to fame he hopes will be delivering a surplus. However, he should be credited for the work he did to almost secure as Energy Minister an agreement between all parties for an emissions and energy policy. This was ultimately rolled when the right wing of his party forced a spill of leadership and Malcom Turnbull was dumped.

Julia Gillard

Julia Gillard became Australia's first female Prime Minister after Kevin Rudd lost in a leadership spill. She was also one of the most successful ones, managing to pass a lot of legislation despite having a hung parliament and relying on independents to get things through. Her biggest lack of success was in getting an emissions policy through and the scheme that was put forward was blocked by the Opposition who thought it unnecessary and strangely by the Greens who said that it didn't go far enough. Her statement that "there will be no carbon tax under the government I lead" gave the opposition all it needed even though her proposal wasn't a tax at all. It was believed that she was a lame duck going into the next election and a spill saw Kevin Rudd return as PM. She is credited for her beginning the Royal Commission into child abuse which saw many changes in society and ultimately the gaoling of priests and even a cardinal, George Pell. Her misogynism speech in parliament in 2012 aimed directly at Tony Abbott was lauded by women and many men all around the world.

Pauline Hanson

Originally elected to the senate in 1996 as an independent after being earlier taken off the Liberal Party ticket because of her racist views, Pauline Hanson is very right wing and accident prone when it comes to speaking and stunts. She lost her seat, was gaoled and then returned to the senate in 2007, this time not targeting Aborigines and Asians in her maiden speech but instead Muslims. She has been able to manipulate governments as her party One Nation has had balance of power opportunities in the Senate. Her party has had members come and go, some being more outlandish, some finding her views and control too hard to take. Her biggest and strangest stunts, gaffes and speeches have included responding to a question on xenophobia with "Please explain?" indicating she didn't know what it meant; wearing a burka into the senate; having her party associated with the NRA; speaking at ultra-right wing rallies; and releasing a video saying that she had been murdered.

<u>Joe Hockey</u>

Joe Hockey served as a minister in the Howard government from 2001 until 2007 and then became treasurer when the Coalition resumed power in 2013. His handling of the treasury portfolio and the 2014 'horror' budget in particular when he described Australians as 'lifters or leaners' saw him lose his portfolio when Malcolm Turnbull became PM. He retired from parliament only to become Australia's ambassador to the US in what seemed a payoff for services not rendered and also something he was not really qualified to do. Nicknamed "Smokin' Joe" by his enemies after he was caught puffing on a huge cigar with Mathias Cormann, this shadow treasurer who claimed that there was a debt and deficit emergency prior to the 2013 election managed to increase that deficit and debt in his short reign as treasurer.

<u>Barnaby Joyce</u>

He started as a senator in 2005 and in 2013 moved to the Lower House. He was often described as the best retail politician in the Coalition but when he became a minister in 2013 and then leader of the Nationals in 2018, things began to go awry. As a senator he threatened to and did cross the floor but as a cabinet minister he was not supposed to. His maverick persona was dulled. From a rural electorate he was supposed to represent what rural people wanted but that wasn't always the case because he towed the Coalition line. Caught up in the dual citizenship issue he had to recontest his seat and was successful. Best known for his ability to shout, his beetroot red face and his extra marital affair that cost him his position, he was one of those who undermined Malcolm Turnbull.

Craig Kelly

A person with strong right-wing views, Craig Kelly wields a lot of power from the backbench. An avid climate change denier and supporter of coal mining, he speaks out on these issues much to the annoyance of his fellow members of the Coalition. He threatened to join the cross bench if he was challenged for preselection and this bullying tactic worked as he was not challenged and held his seat in the 2019 election.

Jacqui Lambie

Jacqui Lambie is a former defence member and was elected to parliament under the Clive Palmer United Party platform as a senator. Following a fall out with Clive Palmer she became an outspoken independent senator who held the balance of power in the Senate. She had to recontest her seat after being found to have dual citizenship and was successful. She shoots straight and from the hip and horse-trades to get her way on many things.

Michael McCormack

He would rather be known as an important politician than an Elvis impersonator, sadly he is good at neither of those. He was the bland leader needed for the Nationals after the demise of Barnaby Joyce. His vacant look and his boring monotone seem to be a genuine reflection of his personality and his Coalition colleagues and indeed the Opposition as well as many members of the public are genuinely concerned when the PM leaves the country and Michael McCormack is left in charge.

<u>Scott Morrison</u>

In 2018, Scott Morrison seemed surprised when all those around him fell and he became Prime Minister. However, some say that it was heavily planned by his supporters. He set up a masterful campaign, creating himself as the person front and centre, and had few policies to criticise thus he was able to narrowly win the unwinnable election in 2019. Having worked in the tourism industry in New Zealand and Australia where he "left" both these positions before his contract was up, he moved into politics in 2007 and made his way quickly into a shadow ministry position. He became Immigration Minister in 2013 introducing sovereign borders policies and denying the media and public to information on asylum seekers and their detention on Christmas Island, Nauru and Manus Island. In 2014 he was moved to Social Services Minister and then when Malcolm Turnbull became PM, Morrison became Treasurer, a position he held until he became Prime Minister. One Question time in Parliament he brought in a lump of coal as a prop and told the Opposition not to be scared of it. His Pentecostal faith he has raised front and centre and this has left him open to criticism. He made horrendous errors of judgement at the end of 2019 and at the beginning of 2020 when the whole east coast of Australia was hit by bushfires. Taking a holiday to Hawaii at the time seemed to show lack of leadership and even on his return his performance was gaffe ridden. A strong supporter of the coal industry and a climate sceptic, he continues to paint a rosy picture of the country's ability to meet emissions targets. Any criticism of him or any of his colleagues he takes the line of "that's just the Canberra bubble" or he obfuscates, changes the topic, won't answer the question or lies. He has earned the nickname as "Scotty from Marketing" but he much prefers Scomo.

<u>Clive Palmer</u>

Clive Palmer first captured the centre of public attention when as a millionaire with mining interests he decided to splash out on building a full-sized working replica of the Titanic in 2012. Before that he opened a dinosaur theme park with huge models overlooking a golf resort. To say that the public thought that he was eccentric was an understatement. They thought much less of him when he had cashflow issues with his nickel business, owing massive tax debts, making a whole lot of workers redundant with wages, redundancies and leave owed and at the same time heavily investing in his quest to become a political player in federal parliament through his newly formed Palmer United Party. He achieved success in the latter and had to be taken to court over the former issues where he sought continual delays and then somehow negotiated deals that were very much in his favour. His PUP rose like a phoenix in 2013 and he became a member of the House of Representatives along with four others who became senators but two soon left his party because of his dictatorial approach. By the time the 2016 election came the phoenix was in ashes. It rose again in the 2018 and one sitting senator from Pauline Hanson's One Nation party defected to the UAP. In the 2019 election, under the banner of the United Australia Party, Palmer invested $60 million and succeeded in swaying voters to the conservative side of politics without any of his candidates winning a seat.

<u>Christopher Pyne</u>

Christopher Pyne came into federal parliament as an MP at the age of 25 in the safe Liberal seat of Sturt. He moved into shadow cabinet in 2008 and when the Coalition came to power in 2013, he became Leader of the House and Minister for Education. He then went on to other ministries before retiring in 2019 having spent 33 years in parliament. He is best known for his dry wit, slightly effeminate voice and for being well liked by all sides of politics. His speed at leaving the chamber when he didn't want to have his vote counted was evident when he and Tony Abbott raced to the doors before they were shut. Christopher proved far too fast for the more athletic Abbott but that was due to his nimble, highly intelligent mind which also left Abbott in its wake.

Kevin Rudd

Kevin Rudd was a Labor leader who had no union affiliations or factions to be beholden to. He had come from the diplomatic corps of the public service and took over as leader of the opposition from the much-liked Kim Beazley in 2006. He took Labor to a landslide win in2007 which saw the sitting Prime Minister, John Howard lose his seat. However, his dictatorial approach to leadership rattled his colleagues and in 2010 Australians woke to find that they had a new PM in Julia Gillard and a new foreign minister in Kevin Rudd. When she looked like facing defeat in 2013 despite having won the 2010 election, she was dumped and Rudd returned as PM in 2013 only to lose the election. Not long after that election Kevin Rudd resigned from parliament. He is best remembered for the apology speech he gave to the indigenous people of Australia and his work in foreign affairs. He remains bitter as to his dumping and regularly adds his voice into the public political discourse.

Bill Shorten

He lost the unlosable election in 2019 because of some very clever campaigning and advertising. As leader of the Opposition for six years until that election he had united the Labor party but hadn't been able to win over the public. His involvement in the removal of Kevin Rudd as PM as well as Julia Gillard as PM didn't help. However, he was a numbers man and had grown up in the union movement and thought he saw the writing on the wall for his party. A Royal Commission into the Union Movement orchestrated by then PM Tony Abbott in an attempt to besmirch Shorten, found no wrongdoing, but it tarnished Shorten's reputation. He is credited with designing the National Disability Insurance Scheme as one of his greatest achievements.

Angus Taylor

The Energy Minister, Angus Taylor has found himself in a lot of hot water. Once seen as future PM material his stocks have fallen low. He has questions to answer on a number of fronts including water buy back schemes where a company he had an interest in made lots of money from the government; doctoring of a document detrimental to the incumbent Sydney Lord Mayor, a position his wife coveted; naming in his maiden speech a well-known author he knew when he was a Rhodes scholar at Oxford even though she wasn't there at the time; possible unlawful land-clearing on his property. As a strong supporter of coal mining he vigorously defends the government stance on the use/misuse of carbon credits left over from over 20 years before to say that targets will be met.

Malcolm Turnbull

A merchant banker and self-made millionaire, Malcolm Turnbull entered parliament in a blue-ribbon liberal seat and rose through the ranks despite him leading the push for a republic. He played the numbers game after the 2007 election and eventually ousted the newly incumbent leader of the Liberal Party, Brendan Nelson. He was too removed from the job because of his stance on the need for action on climate change, by Tony Abbott. Many years later he would replace Abbot as Prime Minister due to the falling popularity of Abbot. In 2016 he took the government to an election win but was ousted once again because of his climate change stance. He eventually retired from politics and his blue-ribbon seat was taken over by an independent for a short period.

Penny Wong

She is the antithesis of what once was the norm in Australian politics. She is educated, well spoken, surprisingly honest, of Asian extraction and a lesbian. Any of these as well as her gender would see her as the target of political bullying, yet she has risen to Labor's Opposition Leader in the Senate because of her stance over many things including the denigration of women. A strong positive advocate in the Marriage Equality debate, she pulls no punches when she needs to call out bullies, spinners of the truth and outright liars. If she was in the House of Representatives and not the Senate, many believe she would become Australia's second female Prime Minister.

The Overseas Characters

<u>Jacinda Ardern</u>
   <u>Boris Johnson</u>
   <u>Kim Jong-un</u>
   <u>Theresa May</u>
   <u>Barack Obama</u>
   <u>Xi Jinping</u>
   <u>Vladimir Putin</u>
   <u>The Royal Family</u>
   <u>Donald Trump</u>

<u>Jacinda Ardern</u>

New Zealand's young PM who gave birth while in office, will be remembered for her humanity, stoicism and honesty in really difficult times. She came to world attention after a shooting massacre which ended up with 51 innocent people dying at mosques. Her warmth and sincerity helped heal the country. She was also exceptional when a number of tourists were killed during a volcanic eruption on White Island. Her independence and willingness to speak from the heart at major leadership conferences has been widely acknowledged.

<u>Boris Johnson</u>

Former Lord Mayor of London, Boris Johnson became known as a blond headed fool who sought the limelight, made extravagant promises that he couldn't deliver. Logic said that he was playing well above his capacity and as is the British way, they elected him as PM replacing Theresa May. His rash promises on Brexit and during the election confirming his position may come back to haunt him.

<u>Kim Jong-un</u>

He is the supreme leader of the poor nation of North Korea that has had a succession of leaders all from the one family. Kim Jong-un's rivals from his family seem to mysteriously pass away or disappear. Rather than spend money of feeding the population, Kim Jong-un has spent money on the development of nuclear weapons and ballistic missiles so that he can become a main player on the world stage. He has attracted the attention of China, Japan and the US in particular who have applied trade and other sanctions on North Korea to keep Kim Jong-un in line. Unfortunately, the impact is far more felt on the poor people of North Korea who now have the state-run media telling them that the country is being victimised and oppressed by these countries so North Korea has to fight back. Kim Jong-un seems very artful in wooing attention and exacting promise in return for ones he has no intention of delivering.

Theresa May

May took on the role as PM after the resignation of David Cameron. She had to fight those in her party and those in the Opposition to try to get somewhere in the ongoing saga that was Brexit. Ultimately, she was tossed out by Boris Johnson who said that he had the solution, but has ended up with less than what May had negotiated.

Barack Obama

Spending two terms as president of the US, Barack Obama was the most statesman like president for many years yet it was the downward turning economy that would see his final term being less fruitful. He constantly had to fight battles with the Republican dominated congress and his health care plan that so many poorer Americans would benefit from was a real struggle. In the end a Republican president would dismantle it almost completely.

Xi Jinping

Xi Jinping is the leader of the most highly populated nation in the world and now as President for Life he continues to bring China closer to being the most powerful country in the world. His belt and road policies in poorer countries where he offers infrastructure for influence are getting developing nations on his side. China's expansion into the South China Sea through the creation of artificial islands has caused diplomatic uproar in other nations but Xi Jinping seems unperturbed by that. Rapid expansion has caused difficulties but China is now no longer a developing nation but a major exporter of goods throughout the world. Xi Jinping keeps a close watch over it all and as the companies are largely state run, his leadership decisions are implemented quite quickly and without question. Hong Kong was drawn back into the Chinese control in 1997 and is an essential element of Chinese access to and influence in world trade and affairs. There are major riots occurring in Hong Kong as people are protesting about the crushing of their freedoms. Xi Jinping may be wanting to avoid another Tiananmen Square situation so they haven't been fully crushed as yet.

Vladimir Putin

He took over as President of Russia from Boris Yeltsin in 2000 and through careful swapping of positions with his colleague Dmitry Medvedev (Prime Minister elected in 2000) Putin has led Russia from 2000 through to now. A fitness fanatic and careful diplomat he has improved the circumstances for many of the people in his country whilst still retaining influence in what were states and satellite countries in the old Soviet Union days. Russian military strength is still evident under Putin but also is the use of cyber attacks on countries where Russia now tries to influence election results, most notably the 2016 election in the US. He has often been seen as backing leaderships in countries that are contrary to the ones the US is backing, Syria is a perfect example. This potentially leads to confrontations between the two super powers of Russia and the US and with a diplomatically unstable President Trump in power, the intelligence and guile of Putin in avoiding a conflict has won out so far.

The Royal Family

The royal family began this period with the strange situation where Prince Phillip was given a knighthood by the Australian Prime Minister, Tony Abbott. There have been royal marriages and births as well as scandals involving Prince Andrew and Prince Phillip. The future king's brother, Harry, now married and with a family has asked that he become independent from the throne as another sign that the monarchy is a frail relic that somehow Australia still wishes to cling to.

Donald Trump

Donald Trump was elected president of the United States in 2016 despite his strange behaviour. He defeated Hilary Clinton after bullying and intimidation and a smear campaign. He somehow managed to do the same thing to other Republican candidates and win the candidacy and then the presidency. He has had a high rotation of staff and has put out fake news and uses twitter to state new policies. After seeming to threaten Ukraine with blackmail in order to get information on his own potential opponent he eventually was impeached by the House. He has been continually mocked by world leaders and has met with the president of North Korea among others in what now appears to be a waste of time. He has withdrawn troops from the Middle East leaving the countries there open for more warfare. He has also pulled out of climate change agreements, trade agreements and nuclear agreements. Lacking diplomacy, economic vision and the ability to communicate with women in particular, he has walked the world stage with the world half in fear that the ignorant spoilt brat of a buffoon may one day begin a nuclear war simply because he can.

The issues

Asylum seekers/Immigration

Australia has had a major issue with asylum seekers. It has taken over five years before so many of them have been processed. They are incarcerated in concentration type camps in foreign countries including on Nauru and Manus Island. These camps have been funded for by Australia but Australia claims no responsibility. It seems it is an out of sight, out of mind policy that is being enacted. At the end of 2018 moves were afoot to allow asylum seekers trapped in concentration camp type conditions to be assessed by independent doctors and if treatment was needed, they were to be transferred to Australia. This was successful but quickly repealed after the May 2019 election.

Banking

The Australian economy remains reliant on the four-pillar banking system. Four privately owned banks, two of which were once owned by the government, remain dominant and the government seems to be at their beck and call. In the Global Financial Crisis of 2007-2008, the government was forced to underwrite these banks because the banks were so intrinsically part of the economy that if one or more failed the nation would fail. These banks because of their size, power and reach were often seen to be making their own rules. After years of being asked, the Coalition finally called a Royal Commission into the banking sector and the rorts were revealed. However, it seems little has changed.

Border Protection

The Australian government dramatically beefed up its border protection after 2013. Special units of armed "Border Force" personnel were formed and some government departments and spy agencies were melded into one super ministry called Home Affairs with special powers and controlled by one minister, Peter Dutton. Australia had gone from a friendly welcoming place to what some people described as a police state. Freedoms were slowly being eroded, including those of the media.

Brexit

In 2016 There was a referendum in Britain about whether Britain should leave the European Union. The Leave vote was heavily reliant on the push factor of immigration and the loss of jobs and didn't really discuss the consequences of such a departure. The Prime Minister David Cameron resigned when the Brexit result was announced. Theresa May was appointed his replacement and set about working through all the conditions to achieve a Brexit deal and avoid some of the ramifications. In the end it cost her her job and she was replaced with Boris Johnson who called an immediate election to ensure that he had the country's backing. Postponement after postponement had taken place since the referendum but a final date was set when a whole new set of border and economic problems would change Britain forever and perhaps disunite the United Kingdom completely as Northern Ireland and Scotland voted to stay in the European Community.

Bushfires

Australia's climate continues to change for the worse. We have always been a place of 'drought and flooding rain'. After years of drought, massive bushfires hit Australia in the last months of 2019 and the early months of 2020 killing many, destroying homes, livestock, forests and wildlife. Many parts of the whole east coast, parts of Tasmania, South Australia and Western Australia were ablaze and attracted worldwide attention and support. Prime Minister Scott Morrison was loudly and strongly condemned for taking a family holiday during that time and not providing the leadership required. Firefighters, mostly volunteers had not had a break for months because the fires were so severe and were unable to be put out. The navy stepped in and rescued people in isolated towns who had fled to the beaches trying to survive. Months and years before government bodies had asked for more money to buy more equipment but the government had denied their request.

China

China's rise to power as a nation has had major implications on trade with Australia and on its diplomatic defence strategies. It is a major importer of our minerals, especially coal, which China consumes 13% of our exports. We, in turn, import 25% of our goods from China. Australia also provides many opportunities in its universities for Chinese students. Concern has been expressed over the purchase of properties, businesses and opportunities by China in Australia and also China's expansion into the South China Sea. There are also signs that politicians have been influenced by Chinese 'gifts'. Senator Sam Dastyari was forced to resign over his links with Chinese moneylenders. At the moment Australia is caught in the middle of a trade war between the US which sees itself as the leader of the world, and the upwardly moving China that will soon dislodge it. Defence ties with the US and trade ties with China make for awkward negotiations for Australian diplomats and politicians especially as the state-owned Chinese company Huawei wish to become involved in the expansion of Australia's telecommunication network.

Climate change

The vast majority of the population acknowledges that there is global warming caused by increased carbon in the atmosphere and that man through its use of fossil fuels contributes heavily to that carbon. There are people in parliament in Australia who deny such things and are at the beck and call of the mining industry. These same right-wing people have controlled any possible position that the Australian government can take to reduce the emissions. Twice Malcolm Turnbull has lost his position because of it, one when he was Prime Minister. Kevin Rudd and Julia Gillard both lost their Prime Ministerships because of the stance and Tony Abbott rose to power because of it. The Coalition government, with a wafer-thin majority could lose power if some of the ultra conservatives withdraw their support. It is a case of a few controlling the vast majority and Australia and the world suffers because of it.

Defence

Australia relies heavily on the US alliances for defence. This has led us into wars however including Vietnam, two Iraqi wars, Afghanistan and against ISIS. The country spends about 2% GDP on defence. In 2020 this is about $40 billion. Very little equipment is made in Australia and our once great shipyards and other defence industries are just shadows of what they used to be. Major contracts have been signed for submarines and planes that will be delivered many years in the future and possibly by then will be out of date and inferior. For many average Australians who see the photo ops of politicians doing their big boys and their toys routine, the expenditure seems unwarranted and money would be better spent on the homeless, reducing the crippling debt that we have. The military in peace time have done us proud in East Timor and assisting with recovery in disaster situations. They remain independent of the government and the Prime Minister is not the Commander in Chief.

Drought

Australia has been enduring more frequent drought periods of late. They are more widespread, lasting longer and having a bigger impact on the country's ability to grow sustainable crops and to farm traditional livestock. There is a growing belief that the foodbowl that we once were, is becoming a thing of the past. Changing away from traditional methods and recognising that there is a water shortage may help stem the flow of farm foreclosures, farmer suicides and small towns shutting up shops. There are rorts in the Murray Darling water catchment and water allocation. Those downstream suffer the most. Droughts are linked to climate change and the federal government has been slow to act. They are more likely to pout an ambulance at the bottom of a cliff than fence off the top of the cliff.

The economy

Australia has a preoccupation with the economy and that drives policy more than the needs of people. We have ever mounting debt and our GDP has fallen because we rely heavily on mining. Our manufacturing industry has all but stalled. Low wage growth, excessive government spending and poorly funded community service programs like aged pension, unemployment benefits and disability and aged care sectors, mean that the people who need help the most become the first casualties of a stagnant economy.

<u>Education</u>

Australian runs a private and state-run school system. The state-run one is supposed to be free and secular, but that is a matter of debate. By comparison the state-run system is poorly funded compared with the private one as federal government funding flows fairly freely to the private system. This has a real bearing on the social strata that lies under the surface of the egalitarian life that Australians believe they have. Introduction of and publication of testing across schools has not properly assessed student outcomes and instead has set up competition between schools and widened the divide between rich and poor schools both in the private and state-run system. Religious groups such as Catholics run separate schools in the private/independent system and are heavily reliant on federal funding. Come election times, whichever party is in power, school funding is used to benefit the party and its ideology. All schools are having less time to do their basic work as more and more of society's ills are blamed on the school system and schools are forced to add "fix-ups" into their curriculum.

<u>Elections</u>

Australians seemed to have a revolving door of Prime Ministers from 2007 onwards. Four times the Prime Ministership was changed without an election. This was very destabilising. After one merry go round ride of Prime Ministers, Tony Abbott swept to power in 2013 only to be part of a domino chain of Prime Ministers leading to Scott Morrison thrust into the position just before an election. He won the unwinnable election by one seat. Many of his counterparts left parliament altogether choosing not to stand rather than lose their seat.

Environment

Australia has a unique environment. It is extremely fragile however and for centuries the indigenous population have managed it. Within the last two centuries since the arrival of Europeans and their land and marine management, there have been massive changes, most of them negative. Entire species of animals have been wiped out and native vegetation has been lost. Heralded all around the world is our Great Barrier Reef but the global warming that has changed the temperature of the water, the use of fertilisers that get washed downstream into the ocean and the introduction of non-native species such as the crown of thorns starfish have decimated a large extent of the reef. Tourism has suffered accordingly. The Reef is a prime example of what is happening across Australia. The Greens political party was set up to provide arguments for a better awareness and management of the environment but they have become just another party, but one of the far left. The public are often left with the feeling of helplessness as the people they elect don't seem to care because the economy is seen to be more important than the environment. Melissa Price was appointed Environment minister by Scott Morrison but had no qualifications apart from a mining background. She made many gaffes and went MIA around election time in 2019.

First Australians

When the Europeans arrived in Australia, they declared the land Terra Nullis indicating that no-one lived there. In doing so, they were stating that the indigenous population were nothing more than fauna, which also meant that the Europeans effectively stole the land from those who had come before them. No treaty such as the one in New Zealand was ever signed. Aborigines became slaves, were conscripted into the army, had their children taken from them to be raised "properly" and were given very few benefits and moved out of productive land. In 1967 they were finally given the right to vote. Under a Labor government in the 1970's they were also allowed to argue for their land rights. For a long period under a conservative government there was little progress made. In 2008 they were finally given a much belated apology about the stolen generation (children taken from their families). In 2017, the celebrated Statement from the Heart was made recommending changes to the way the indigenous population could have a voice about their future. The Coalition government rejected it out of hand.

Leadership

Australia had been devoid of strong leadership since around 1996 in the early days of John Howards prime ministership both in opposition and government at a federal level. The state governments had a number of effective progressive leaders in that time but there was not the quality coming through at a federal level who were willing and capable of leading. Some were trapped in the senate and couldn't become a prime minister. With so many factions in the major parties, would be leaders needed to spend more time unifying their party than unifying the nation. Oppositions and governments were at loggerheads just to prove that there was a point of difference. The image of politicians and indeed leaders went on a downward spiral and may not have bottomed out yet.

Marriage Equality/Gender Equity

The idea that LGBTQI people should be able to legally marry had been the bone of contention for a long long time. Some states wished to make it happen but were wary because the federal government had power to override state laws. It was determined that a law had to be enacted federally to guarantee people the rights that others took for granted. There were all sorts of delaying mechanisms put in place by right wing parliamentarians, media shock jocks and by religious groups. One of these was the introduction of a plebiscite which was a very expensive, non-binding and unnecessary act to slow down the momentum. It was very divisive, yet in the end proved to the politicians that the vast majority of Australians wanted marriage equality to happen. The passing of the law on Marriage Equality was celebrated by LGBTQI and heterosexuals alike and the ultra-conservative politicians when asked to vote in parliament defied their constituents by abstaining or voting no. They proved to be only a minority.

The Media

The media in Australia used to be quite diverse and rules were put in place so that no one person or media company could dominate. However, under changes by the Coalition these rules were relaxed and the Newscorp companies have begun to dominate print, radio and television media, squeezing out the smaller players. The owners of large media companies have extraordinary access to and influence on politicians and policies of parties. Rupert Murdoch is one of the owners who has more say than most. Politicians have been stretching "in confidence" aspects of the law to stop or delay Freedom of Information requests by journalists and when information has been released it has often been heavily redacted. Pressure has been placed on journalists and media groups to reveal sources through the use of Federal Police. Politicians however use the media for the purpose of deliberately leaking of information and have become very fussy whom they will be interviewed by on radio and television. Door stop interviews to create sound bites suitable for the evening news are often held but politicians are finding it difficult to adapt to the 24-hour news cycle and the rise of social media.

Middle East

The Middle East has been a hot bed of uncertainty and division from the earliest of times, some of it religious based, most of it economic. With the rise of the need for oil products, it became and remains a powder keg. At the end of World War 1 artificial lines were drawn on a map separating tribes and families. At the end of the Second World War there was a need to create a Jewish state and the nation of Israel further divided the area. War after war has been fought non-stop between a host of nations. Interference by multinationals and backed by European and US governments has not helped. The ever-present threat of a nuclear holocaust exists and when one renegade Arab group took on the US on US soil causing the 9/11 events, the world held its collective breath. Strategic withdrawal of US European and Russian troops seems unlikely as this led to the rise of other groups such as Al-Qaeda and ISIS. Underlying all this is the world's need for petroleum-based products.

North Korea

This poor impoverished reclusive nation has been under the rule of one family since 1948. Money is spent on developing nuclear capabilities and missiles to strike countries. Surrounded by China, Russia and South Korea, its leaders have been able to get the population to believe that they are under imminent attack. Widely seen as a renegade state, it manages to strut a high profile and threaten countries around it.

Religious Freedoms

Australia has a good set of discrimination laws despite it not actually having a bill of rights. After the religious community were rolled in the Marriage Equality discussion, plebiscite and vote, voices were raised about enshrining discriminatory rights for religions into law. Australia is supposed to have a separation between church and state, through secular governments. This is more in name than in deed as the religious lobby groups wield a lot of power and influence despite a steep decline in the number of people practising any religion. The Coalition government has been pushing for a revamp of the religious discrimination laws to allow religious bodies to have special dispensation to discriminate.

Russia

Since the end of the Cold War in 1991, Russia has loomed large in Australia's foreign affairs as Australia walks a tightrope of increasing its trade with Russia but also aware of Russia's expansion plans through influencing other countries. Tony Abbott once threatened to "shirtfront" Vladimir Putin over Russian involvement in the downing of a plane and its use naval ships north of Australia. Abbott had no idea what shirtfront really meant. Putin laughed it off and Australia went down in Russian estimation. Because of our close defence ties with the US, Australia has often been drawn into issues that involve Russia.

Unemployment/Employment

Financial support for those unemployed has waned and many people are struggling. Rules on statistics have been changed and there is a steady increase in the underemployed. With a stroke of a pen, someone working one hour per week is considered employed. Newstart is an allowance given to the unemployed to support them when seeking new jobs. Those on these benefits must be actively seeking employment, even if there is none or they lose the benefits. They become easy targets for politicians and the media and named as dole bludgers. For many people particularly in rural regions there aren't jobs available and this causes an exodus to the city as it is difficult to survive on the allowance given. Australian manufacturing has all but shut down completely. There is a large amount of automation in many work places and that means that fewer people are needed. With a large pool of people to choose from, employers are able to suppress wages too. Traditional jobs gone, little change in education to expand opportunities, low wage growth and a very low unemployment benefit, young people cannot get into the job market and housing market. This just further stagnates the economy.

Unions

There has been a dramatic decline in union membership in Australia to the extent that the Labor Party, the traditional voice of the unions in parliament are losing their base and are being forced to look elsewhere. Many unions have become political and dominated by trying to achieve political ideological gains rather than act in the best interest of their members. This has led to the disenfranchisement of members and the loss of membership. However, the biggest change has been due to the Coalition government's push to undermine unions and change labour laws.

World trade

Countries and groups of nations have put in trade tariffs and barriers to protect their own producers. However, because there is a supply and demand backbone to all their economies, and multinational companies, governments have been trying to reach individual agreements between countries. Some of these are symbolic and trade can see the dumping of cheap or excess products which greatly affect an individual nation. Cheap labour in some countries undercuts others. Scarcity of one commodity can affect the capacity of another. There is no level playing field as countries try to woo individual companies with lucrative tax deals. China has entered the market and is now a powerful player and the once dominant US is finding it difficult to lose its stranglehold on world markets.

Return to Contents page